P9-AOG-112

$ 5.00

# Contents

# Conrad's Early Sea Fiction

## *The Novelist as Navigator*

Paul Bruss

Lewisburg: Bucknell University Press
London: Associated University Presses

© 1979 by Associated University Presses, Inc.

Associated University Presses, Inc.
Cranbury, New Jersey 08512

Associated University Presses
Magdalen House
136– 148 Tooley Street
London SE1 2TT, England

**Library of Congress Cataloging in Publication Data**

Bruss, Paul, 1943-
   Conrad's early sea fiction.

   Bibliography: p.
   Includes index.
1. Conrad, Joseph, 1857-1924—Criticism and interpretation. 2. Sea
stories—History and criticism. 3. Navigation in literature. I. Title.
PR6005.04Z5676    823'.9'12    77-74402
ISBN 0-8387-2133-8

PRINTED IN THE UNITED STATES OF AMERICA

# Conrad's Early Sea Fiction

*for Kath*

# Preface

This study examines the nature and the significance of Conrad's use of navigational metaphor in his early sea fiction from *The Nigger of the "Narcissus"* to "The End of the Tether," from 1897 to 1902. That navigational metaphor is a primary ingredient in this fictional period is not the question. Every reader of Conrad knows how pervasively his long career as seaman-captain influenced both theme and metaphor throughout his writing of fiction. One need remember only "Youth" from the early period or *The Shadow-Line* from a later one in order to recognize that the rise to the status of navigator remains a metaphoric constant in Conrad's fiction. Navigational metaphor, however, involves more than the process of initiation or a rise to new stature. This study, although not focused upon explaining the nuances of nautical situations and their appropriate terminology, exposes and elaborates upon some of the fundamental professional and sometimes metaphysical assumptions that underlie Conrad's use of navigational metaphor. As such a study, it possesses a distinct advantage over the customary thematic analysis of "initiation" in Conrad's sea fiction: it defines the major aesthetic problems in Conrad's first coherent period of writing and thus makes accessible the more intricate, artistic relationships among the eight principal tales in the period.

P.B.

# Acknowledgments

I am greatly indebted to two former teachers, Bruce Johnson and George Ford (both of whom read and commented on the original manuscript), for their generous encouragement and consideration. Maurice Beebe read the final manuscript and offered a number of helpful suggestions for which I am also grateful. During the long months of rethinking and revision, my wife, Kath, provided the daily encouragement and support, and thus it is to her that the book is dedicated.

I wish to thank the following publishers for having given me permission to quote from published works:

*College Literature*, for permission to use a modified version of my article "Conrad's 'Youth': Problems of Interpretation," 1 (1973): 218–29.

*Conradiana*, for permission to use a modified version of my article "*Lord Jim:* The Maturing of Marlow," 8 (1976):13–26.

Doubleday & Company, Inc., for permission to reprint excerpts from the following works by Joseph Conrad: *Almayer's Folly; Last Essays,* Copyright 1925 by Doubleday & Company, Inc.; *Lord Jim; The Mirror of the Sea; The Nigger of the "Narcissus"; Notes on Life and Letters,* Copyright 1921 by Doubleday & Company, Inc.; *A Personal Record; Tales of Unrest; Typhoon;* and *Youth.*

W. W. Norton & Company, Inc., for permission to quote from Joseph Conrad, *Heart of Darkness,* Norton Critical Edition, 1971.

*Studies in the Novel,* for permission to use a modified version of my article "Marlow's Interview with Stein: The Implications of the Metaphor," 5 (1973):491–503.

*Studies in Short Fiction,* for permission to use a modified version of my article " 'The End of the Tether': Teleological Diminishing in Conrad's Early Metaphor of Navigation," 13 (1976):311–20.

*Studies in the Twentieth Century,* for permission to use a modified version of my article "Lord Jim and the Metaphor of Awakening," 14 (1974):69–89.

# Conrad's Early Sea Fiction

# 1

# Conrad's Essays: The Background behind His Early Sea Fiction

One particularly beneficial, and yet to this point neglected, approach to Conrad's early sea fiction is to isolate the author's own comments, in his four volumes of essays, concerning navigation.[1] It is true that these volumes appear after 1902: *The Mirror of the Sea* in 1906, *A Personal Record* in 1912, *Notes on Life and Letters* in 1921, and *Last Essays* in 1926.[2] It is also true that, unlike *The Mirror of the Sea,* the other three volumes (and especially the last two) contain long reflections upon Conrad's attitudes toward other writers and their works. Neither reservation, however, need dissuade Conrad's readers from relying upon all four volumes in order to define the deeply entrenched attitudes that largely determine the course of his early sea fiction. For as V. S. Naipaul observed at a recent commemoration of Conrad's death,

> Conrad, when he settled down to write, was . . . a man whose character had been formed. He knew his world, and had reflected on his experience. Solitariness, passion, the abyss: the themes are constant in Conrad. There is a unity in a writer's work; but the Conrad who wrote *Victory*, though easier and more direct in style, was no more experienced and wise than the Conrad who, twenty years before, had written *Almayer's Folly*.[3]

Such a comment eloquently points up the probable consistency of attitude toward navigation throughout Conrad's writing career. Given the fact that he enjoyed a very successful career as a seaman and that he was already forty years old when he began publishing his sea fiction, one need not hesitate to expropriate comments from even the very last essays in order to establish the fundamental assumptions behind Conrad's early use of navigational metaphor. Indeed, when isolated from Conrad's fiction, these four volumes of essays achieve a most striking unity of perspective precisely because of their frequent reference to the matters of seamanship—matters that, for Conrad, must remain constant. In lieu of a biographical discussion of Conrad's career as a seaman, then, these volumes of essays help me isolate, first, Conrad's reflections upon his own initiations at sea and, second, the major attitudes that underlie his reflecting and, presumably, his fictionalizing upon life at sea.

That past initiations at sea are very important to a seaman of Conrad's stature is probably not surprising. What does give one pause is the fact that much later in his life, having become a successful novelist as well as a seaman of the first order, Conrad still smarted from the incredulousness that his initial decision (at fifteen) ''to go to sea'' occasioned:

> At first, like those sounds that, ranging outside the scale to which men's ears are attuned, remain inaudible to our sense of hearing, this declaration passed unperceived. It was as if it had not been. Later on, by trying various tones, I managed to arouse here and there, a surprised momentary attention—the ''What was that funny noise? What an extraordinary outbreak!'' Presently a wave of scandalised astonishment . . . stirred up a mass of remonstrance, indignation, pitying wonder, bitter irony and downright chaff. I could hardly breathe under its weight and certainly had no words for an answer. (*PR*, pp. 41–42)

From the beginning of the acknowledgment of his desire to go to sea the young Conrad endured a long period of moral ambivalence as his elders and peers all sought to deflect him from the pursuit of such an end. Shortly thereafter, for example, while touring the continent during the summer of 1873, Conrad engaged in endless argument with his tutor, Mr. Pulman, about the unusual and inadequate nature of his desire. Again the elder Conrad vividly remembered the pressure of the tutor's skepticism: ''What reward could I expect from such a life at the end of my years, either in ambition, honour or conscience?'' (*PR*, p. 43). The young Conrad, nevertheless, perhaps because he was ''an incorrigible, hopeless Don Quixote'' (*PR*, p. 44), prevailed in his determination and launched a career at sea without the enthusiastic support of his family or of the influential community to which his family belonged.

The crucial aspect of Conrad's determination is the fact that as a very young man he thoroughly divorced himself from the aristocratic traditions of his family, traditions that he profoundly respected, and heeded instead his inner longing for the sea. It is in this light that his first self-realizations at sea achieve their greatest significance. To be sure, from December 1874 to February 1877, while under the general sponsorship of the wealthy French banker-shipper M. Delestang and while sailing three times to the West Indies (first as a passenger, then as an apprentice seaman, and finally as steward), Conrad seems to have experienced little initiation of consequence.[4] In fact, it was only after arguing with his sponsor and ignoring his short career in French merchant ships that he became conscious of any significant change in personal attitude. Having then joined a syndicate of four who purchased a felucca of sixty tons, the *Tremolino*, in order to smuggle guns from Marseilles to the Carlist guerillas in Catalonia, Spain, he himself (between March and December 1877) made several voyages in the Mediterranean, "the nursery of our navigating ancestors," and there learned two things: "to walk in the ways of my craft and [to] grow in the love of the sea" (*MS*, p. 155). Both lessons, by awakening the restless Conrad to a new way of life, eased the moral distress that his separation from the aristocratic heritage of his family three years earlier had occasioned and that his troubled service under M. Delestang had hardly diminished. It is for this reason that, many years later, he acknowledged that the *Tremolino* had "given [him] everything": "I owe to her the awakened love for the sea that . . . stole into my heart with a sort of gentle violence, and brought my imagination under its despotic sway" (*MS*, p. 157). This awakening was the virtual beginning of Conrad's mature devotion to the sea.

Even then, however, it was not until early 1881, four years and five ships later, while enjoying his first berth as officer (as third mate) on the *Loch Etive*,[5] that Conrad endured a moment of crisis that because of its attendant exposure to the broad tradition of seamanship, he would later regard as one of the major moral watersheds of his career. In an essay entitled "Initiation" Conrad describes a mid-Atlantic rescue of nine men from a Danish brig that was seriously damaged by a hurricane during her return from the West Indies. The immediate occasion for the reminiscence is Conrad's general discussion of the "unfathomable cruelty" of the sea, but generally the episode—especially under the dramatic force of Conrad's imagination—centers upon the self-realization that the young third mate enjoys. In the narrative Conrad repeatedly recounts how he is warned by his captain to be careful with his lifeboat, and how, probably because he possesses no previous experience as an officer, he scorns that caution much as if he believes himself ready for whatever demands a rescue might create. The upshot is that the inexperienced mate must learn from his own, somewhat haphazard, managing of the circumstances. He does. He brings his boat quickly to the brig, virtually rescues the brig's captain by himself, and then watches the desperate escape of the two terrified men who had remained at the brig's pumps. For Conrad it is this scene of final desperation that is revolutionary: "The cynical indifference of the sea to the merits of human suffering and courage, laid bare in this ridiculous, panic-tainted performance extorted from the dire extremity of nine good and honourable seamen, revolted me" (*MS*, pp. 141–42). Such a revelation deprives the third mate of the precious illusions concerning the sea's "enchanting charm" that his *Tremolino* days had fostered. He may still possess a fascination for the sea, but he knows that in this experience he has "become a seaman at last" (*MS*, p. 142) in the sense that his earlier romantic enthusiasms now know the seasoning of responsible seamanship. While listening to the exhausted captain's appreciative oration over his sinking brig, he fully realizes the glory of the seaman's tradition:

> [The brig] had lived, [the captain] had loved her: she had suffered, and he was glad she was at rest. It was an excellent discourse. And it was orthodox, too, in its fidelity to the cardinal article of a seaman's faith, of which it was a single-minded confession. "Ships are all right." They are. They who live with the sea have got to hold by that creed first and last. (*MS*, pp. 146–47)

In this moment of crisis Conrad discovered for himself one of the true bases for the traditions of the sea—the faithful devotion to one's ship—and it was this discovery that underlay his statement, years later, that upon reaching his own captain, who was now smiling with "pathetic indulgence," he had "completed the cycle of [his] initiation" (*MS*, p. 147). In his own eyes he had now been rooted not only in a profound love for the sea but also in the purposes and the traditions of seamanship.

Conrad's successful achievement of the necessary credentials for commanding in the Merchant Service was also an occasion for some initiation. In his discussion of that achievement, in fact, Conrad virtually turns the three examinations before the Marine Department of the Board of Trade into a series of harrowing experiences. The first examination, for example, lasts "for hours, for hours," with "a sense of untold ages having been spent . . . on mere preliminaries" (*PR*, p. 113), and under such pressure Conrad feels his brain becoming "addled," his thoughts "queer." The second examination, while it lasts for only forty minutes, also proves to be an outrage, full of "implacable animosity" and difficult questions of procedure, and again Conrad feels an exasperation almost beyond endurance. After both examinations, however, he is supremely conscious of "walk[ing] on air along Tower Hill, where so many good men had lost their heads, because, I suppose, they were not resourceful enough to save them" (*PR*, pp. 116–17). With his already strong sense of purpose and tradition, awakened in such episodes as on the *Loch Etive,* Conrad is himself very resourceful, and thus he succeeds where many sailors before him (as well as the many men condemned to the Tower) had failed. After the exasperations of the first two, the third examination for master proves easy. For then, while the examiner reminisces about bits from his own life at sea, Conrad suddenly exults in the significance of his adoption as master into a long tradition of responsibility: "This examiner . . . awaken[ed] in me the sense of the continuity of that sea-life *into which I had stepped from outside:* giving a touch of human intimacy to the machinery of official relations. I felt adopted. His experience was for me, too, as though he had been an ancestor" (*PR*, p. 118; emphasis added). In this discussion of his professional examinations Conrad's emphasis is clearly upon his absorption into a tradition outside his childhood experience. That emphasis now bears further elaboration.

That Conrad should have prized his initiation into a long and rich tradition outside his childhood experience is understandable if one realizes how difficult it must have been for him to reject the aristocratic traditions of his family upon leaving Poland. In a very late essay entitled "Tradition," while writing appreciatively of the devotion displayed by the British Merchant Service during World War I, Conrad comments upon why his initiation into the traditions of navigation retained so much significance throughout his life: "It is perhaps because I have not been *born* to the inheritance of that tradition, which has yet fashioned the fundamental part of my character in my young days, that I am so consciously aware of it and venture [in March 1918] to vindicate its existence in this out-spoken manner" (*NLL*, p. 196). On the basis of this comment it is easy to infer that the traditions of the Merchant Service had a profound effect upon the young Conrad precisely because they replaced the aristocratic traditions of his family. In another essay, "Well Done," written shortly thereafter, Conrad makes such an inference more than probable. Discussing his fictional creation of characters belonging to the service, he insists:

> I have written of them with all the truth that was in me, and with all the impartiality of which I was capable. Let me not be misunderstood in this statement. . . . I have looked upon them with a jealous eye, expecting perhaps even more than it was strictly fair to expect. And no wonder — since I had elected to be one of them very deliberately, very completely, without any looking back or looking elsewhere. The circumstances were such as to give me the feeling of complete identification, a very vivid comprehension that *if I wasn't one of them I was nothing at all.* (*NLL*, pp. 182-83; emphasis added)

Here the importance of the service tradition in resolving Conrad's earlier difficulties of moral ambivalence becomes unmistakable. Indeed, because it provided Conrad with a solid foundation of principles and responsibilities at the very time when not only his own life but the Western world was generally falling prey to the paralyzing crises of epistemology and of ethics inherent in the work of such thinkers as Nietzsche and Freud, it actually became his insurance for a life of action, of moral resolve, of heady accomplishment. The tradition of seamanship, therefore, must serve as a primary key to all of Conrad's experience at sea and, presumably, to all his fiction about the sea.

Throughout his years as officer at sea Conrad became ever more conscious of the importance of the ideals and the achievements that have guided sailors' experience throughout the ages. In a sense, however, it was not such experiences as he had on the *Loch Etive* but Conrad's own childhood that ultimately accounts for his thorough adoption of this adventurous tradition. For even while very young, as several of his essays point out, he found himself attracted to geography, especially to the worlds of the polar and the African explorers.[6] Later in life, of course, after having become a seaman and then a novelist, Conrad revealed an even deeper admiration and respect for geography than had characterized his childhood. In one of his last essays, "Geography and Some Explorers," for example, Conrad applauds the efforts, say, of a Columbus or of a Balboa, each of whom sailed under a navigational difficulty of the extreme: "They could calculate their latitude, but the problem of longitude was a matter which bewildered their minds and often falsified their judgment" (*LE*, p. 7). This problem, when coupled with "the dangers of unknown seas" and "the awful geographical incertitudes" of the era, understandably impresses upon Conrad the true greatness of such navigators as Captain Cook in the Pacific and Sir John Franklin in the Arctic—or of any navigator who devoted his life to furthering man's knowledge of the sea under rudimentary conditions. As a sailor of the wide seas himself, Conrad savors the subtleties of navigational achievements, and toward the end of this essay on geography he relates an incident from his own life—while he was captain of the *Otago* in 1888—that puts such savoring in a special light.

Conrad recounts how one day, facing a voyage from Sydney to Mauritius, "all the deep-lying historic sense of the exploring adventures in the Pacific surged up to the surface of [his] being" (*LE*, p. 18). The surging prompts him to consult his owners about the possibility of reaching Mauritius "by way of Torres Strait," a passage named after a seventeenth-century Spaniard who did not realize that New Guinea lined one side of the strait and Australia the other, and thus a passage "whose true contours were . . . [first] laid down on the map by James Cook, the navigator without fear and without reproach" (*LE*, p. 19). What appeals to Conrad, here, is the chance to recover some of the old navigators' spirit. The *Otago*'s owners warn him that the summer sailing season may be too far advanced — they fear that the *Otago* will suffer a period of severe calm in the strait — but Conrad is not to be denied. Because the season is advanced, he avoids further delay and insists on leaving Sydney "during a heavy southeast gale." Nine days later he reaches the strait and there, "not without a certain emotion," he packs on the *Otago* "every bit of canvas she could carry" (*LE*, p. 20). Ominously, two wrecked ships, the *Honolulu* and a nameless American ship, define the beginning and the end of the passage, but an enraptured Conrad unhesitatingly directs his ship through the strait in only thirty-six hours (nine of them spent in anchor at night). Outside the passage, recognizing an island — for him it is "a hallowed spot" — where Captain Cook had gone ashore in a gesture that ended his 1762 voyage of expedition on the *Endeavour*, Conrad communes with his ancestor:

> I could depict to myself the famous seaman navigator, a lonely figure in a three-cornered hat and square-skirted lace coat, pacing to and fro slowly on the rocky shore, while in the ship's boat, lying off on her oars, the coxswain kept his eyes open for the slightest sign of the captain's hand. (*LE*, p. 21)

Outside Torres Strait a proud Conrad savors his own, although vicarious, participation in the richest dimension of his chosen tradition, and thereafter (even at the end of his life) he can only marvel over the inclusion of such a privilege: "What would the memory of my sea life have been for me if it had not included a passage through Torres Strait, in its fullest extent, from the mouth of the great Fly River right on along the track of the early navigators?" (*LE*, p. 19). Presumably, the memory would still have been great. The experience in Torres Strait, however, by defining him as navigator in the best sense of the tradition, turns Conrad into one of the possessors of "a spark of the sacred fire" (*LE*, p. 21).[7]

Conrad, then, throughout his career as seaman, handled the moral ambivalence that resulted from the rejection of his family's aristocratic tradition by becoming a master in the British Merchant Service and thus by accepting for himself the principles and attitudes of seamanship. He had known at age twenty on the *Tremolino*, or at twenty-three aboard the *Loch Etive*, or at twenty-nine when he gained his master's certificate, or even at thirty-one when he sailed through Torres Strait the marvelous sense of initiation into a rich tradition of imagination and devotion, and such initiation went a long way toward vindicating his abrupt departure from Poland. He may, to be sure, have known other initiations, such as those recounted in "Youth" and *Heart of Darkness* and "Falk: A Reminiscence," but the essential point is clear: it was Conrad's thorough and successful participation in the tradition of seamanship that enabled him to become the possessor, and even the artist, of a profound modern vision.

Conrad's career as a seaman affected both the content and the form of his early fiction. I shall have something to say about the latter at the end of this chapter. Here I wish to treat the matter of content—the three major attitudes behind Conrad's use of the navigational metaphor from 1897 to 1902: (1) the supremacy of sails to steam, (2) sailing as a fine art and tradition, and (3) the significance of work as salvation.

The first attitude, obviously rooted in Conrad's own experience, has received very little critical attention. In an essay unfinished at his death, "Legends," Conrad points out that the final heyday of sailing ships lasted only sixty years, from 1850 to 1910, and he concludes: "The pathos of that era lies in the fact that when the sailing ships and the art of sailing them reached their perfection, they were already doomed" (*LE*, p. 46). Conrad himself, sailing from 1874 to 1894, must have been conscious throughout his career of the continued decline of sailing. When he gained his master's certificate on November 10, 1886, for example, he heard his examiner tell him: "You will go into steam presently. Everybody goes into steam" (*PR*, p. 117). But Conrad did not. Except for steaming eight weeks aboard the *Mavis* in 1878, seven weeks aboard the *Europa* during the winter of 1879–80, four months aboard the *Vidar* late in 1887, seven weeks aboard the *Roi des Belges* on the Congo River during 1890, and seven weeks aboard the ill-fated *Adowa* during the winter of 1893–94,[8] Conrad managed to develop his career under the graceful sails of fourteen schooners and barques. In fact, while he (perhaps unconsciously) limited his average tenure on a steamer to only nine or ten weeks, he usually enjoyed long (sometimes well over a year) periods of uninterrupted service aboard his sailing ships. That he was not comfortable in steam service is, therefore, a likely inference. If one recalls how he abruptly quit his position on the *Vidar* on January 5, 1888, and quickly fled the *Roi des Belges* in 1890 because of a gripping illness, one may even conclude that Conrad did not possess the disposition for service in steam. Later in life Conrad demeaned this reluctance to serve in steam by commenting: "I never went into steam — not really. If I only live long enough I shall become a bizarre relic of a dead barbarism, a sort of monstrous antiquity, the only seaman of the dark ages who had never gone into steam — not really" (*PR*, p. 117). That this comment is facetious, however, is probably clear enough. One only need refer again to Conrad's discussion of sailing through Torres Strait in order to illustrate the fact that he strongly preferred service in sails precisely because it was that service that associated him intimately with the old world of explorers and discoverers.[9]

As one might expect, such a thorough appreciation of the world of sails frequently leads Conrad to demean steam service on many counts. He may, for example, underscore his own preference by stressing the calm of a sailing ship: "There are neither vibrations nor mechanical noises to grow actively wearisome" (*LE*, p. 25). Or, admitting that sailing ships, too, are machinery, he asserts that such ships at least do their work with economy — "in perfect silence and with a motionless grace, . . . taking nothing away from the material stores of the earth" (*MS*, p. 37). Or, acknowledging that both sailing ships and steamers can lose their means of movement, he suggests: "Of all ships disabled at sea, a steamer who has lost her propeller is the most helpless. . . . a sailing-vessel with her lofty spars gone is to look upon a defeated but indomitable warrior" (*MS*, p. 63). The use of the appreciative warrior metaphor accurately reveals how thoroughly committed Conrad was to his past vocation in sails. He grants the steamer nothing, and even though the steamer has promoted regularity and innovations in shipping and sea travel, he actually begrudges her such important advances. On the subject of shipping, for example, Conrad demeans the loading of cargo into a steamer, an act that was once "a matter of skill, judgment, and knowledge": "The modern steamship with her many holds is not loaded. . . . She is filled up. Her cargo is not stowed in any sense; it is simply dumped into her . . .,with clatter and hurry and racket and heat, in a cloud of steam and a mess of coal-dust" *(MS*, p. 47). Furthermore, just as the act of stevedoring has disappeared, so — Conrad insists — the art of ocean travel has suffered a cruel blow. Because the traveler on a sailing ship of necessity becomes "acclimatized to that moral atmosphere of ship life which he [is] fated to breathe for so many days" *(LE*, p. 36), he gradually displays an interest in and a sympathy for the activities of the sailors serving him. The result is that he achieves a true vacation, a total rest from his land cares. The fixing of a definite arrival date for the new steamer-hotels, however, has destroyed that luxury: "That every passenger [on a steamer] wishes to escape there can be not the slightest doubt. He may say what he likes, but . . . he looks forward to his release much as any prisoner. The modern traveller has never the time to get into an acquiescent mood" *(LE*, p. 36). According to Conrad, then, the modern traveler, despite the opulence and convenience of the steamer's fittings, possesses very little, if any, advantage over his forebears.

In all these quotations, a brief selection, Conrad's fundamental belief in the superiority of sails is unmistakable. These passages, however, are merely incidental. In an essay written in 1912, "The Loss of the *Titanic*," Conrad isolates a problem that illuminates a more serious basis for his devotion to sails. Addressing the question of why the *Titanic*'s sinking occasioned so much surprise and dismay, Conrad writes:

> You build a 45,000 ton hotel of thin steel plates to secure the patronage of, say, a couple of thousand rich people. . . you decorate it in the style of the Pharaohs or in the Louis Quinze style — I don't know which — and then please the aforesaid fatuous handful of individuals, who have more money than they know what to do with, and to the applause of two continents, you launch that mass with 2,000 people on board at twenty-one knots across the sea — *a perfect exhibition of the modern blind trust in mere material and appliances.* And then this happens. General uproar. The blind trust in material and appliances has received a terrible shock. *(NLL*, p. 218; emphasis added)

Two years later, in "Protection of Ocean Liners," Conrad reaffirmed his point: "We have been accustoming ourselves to put our trust in material, technical skill, invention, and scientific contrivances to such an extent that we have come at last to believe that with these things we can overcome the immortal gods themselves. Hence when a disaster... happens, there arises, besides the shock to our humane sentiments, a feeling of irritation" (*NLL*, pp. 250–51). The scathing irony in both passages exposes the nature of Conrad's real quibble with steamers. Such ships falsify man's normal relations with the universe of contingency. Instead of recognizing his limitations, the sailor (or passenger) in steam becomes conscious only of his supposed power over the universe.

Conrad's second major attitude, the view of sailing as a fine art, is inherent in his strong preference for sails over steam. One might argue about which came first, Conrad's devotion to sailing ships or his appreciation of sailing as a fine art, but ultimately Conrad seems to argue that it is the devotion to the ships that is the basis for the art. Early in *The Mirror of the Sea*, for example, while exploring the nature of the relationship between the sailing ship and her seaman, Conrad suggests: "You must treat with an understanding consideration the mysteries of [your ship's] feminine nature, and then she will stand by you faithfully in the unceasing struggle with forces wherein defeat is no shame. . . . She has her rights as though she could breathe and speak. . . . A ship is not a slave" (*MS*, p. 56). In a later essay, "Well Done," Conrad makes even more definitive his view of the ship's role in awakening the seaman's devotion and moral purpose: "What awakens the seaman's duty, what lays that impalpable constraint upon the strength of his manliness, what commands his not always dumb if always dogged devotion, is not the spirit of the sea but something that in his eyes has a body, a character, a fascination, and almost a soul — it is his ship" (*NLL*, p. 191). It is evident in both passages that it is the necessary devotion to the ship that constitutes for Conrad "the best and most genuine part" of a sailor's life. He believes, in fact, that because "you must make [your ship] easy in a seaway, [because] you must never forget that you owe her the fullest share of your thought, of your skill, of your self-love" (*MS*, p. 56), the ship can hardly avoid turning the devotion of her men into a fine art whose character is beyond reproach: "The art of handling ships is finer, perhaps, than the art of handling men" (*MS*, p. 28). To be sure, because it is the devotion to a sailing ship, not to a steamer, that serves for Conrad as the key to the sailor's self-realization, he here finds himself in possession of even more reason to disparage the recent advances in navigational technology. He knows that there is an essential difference between the seamen of yesterday who sailed and the seamen of tomorrow who steam, and for him that difference ultimately leads to a lamentation over the dying of his art: "History repeats itself, but the special call of an art which has passed away is never reproduced. It is as utterly gone out of the world as the song of a destroyed wild bird. Nothing will awaken the same response of pleasurable emotion or conscientious endeavour" (*MS*, p. 30). The appearance of steamers, according to Conrad, thrust the art of sailing into the "Valley of Oblivion." During his own years at sea, nevertheless, Conrad himself knew the highest qualities of that art.

Perhaps the most important dimension of Conrad's view of sailing as a fine art is his appreciation of the tradition behind the art. Merely by virtue of vocation all sailors, according to Conrad, "belong to one family: all are descended from that adventurous and shaggy ancestor who . . . accomplished the first coasting trip in a sheltered bay ringing with the admiring howls of his tribe" (*MS*, pp. 148–49). Beyond vocation, however, there is also the matter of the sailors' skill or craft, which Conrad regards as the "redeeming and ideal aspect" of their industry. He associates this fine ideal with tradition:

> Such skill, the skill of technique, is more than honesty: it is something wider, embracing honesty and grace and rule in an elevated and clear sentiment, not altogether utilitarian, which may be called the honour of labour. It is made up of accumulated tradition, kept alive by individual pride, rendered exact by professional opinion, and, like the higher arts, it is spurred on and sustained by discriminating praise. (*MS,* p. 24)

Here the tradition of sailing, particularly its contemporary fostering by professional opinion and praise, functions as another primary goad to the development of the sailors' craft and skill. Like the personality of a ship, the tradition behind the fine art of sailing raises sailors "above the frailties of their dead selves" (*NLL,* p. 183) and thus presents the opportunity for further self-realization:

> All ideals are built on the ground of solid achievement, which in a given profession creates in the course of time a certain tradition, or, in other words, a standard of conduct. The existence of a standard of conduct in its turn makes the most improbable achievement possible, by augmenting the power of endurance and of self-sacrifice amongst

men who look to the past for their lessons and for their inspiration. (*LE,* p. 58)

In this passage from a very late essay Conrad admires tradition not merely as a conservative ethic by which a seaman's skill may be judged but also as the basis both for the reaffirmation of well-established skills and for the self-realization that can be truly creative and innovative. Throughout Conrad's early sea fiction, therefore, it is not surprising that the tradition behind the art of sailing serves at least as important a force in sailors' lives as the necessary devotion to a ship.

The third attitude behind Conrad's use of navigational metaphor is, perhaps, the most basic: the sailor's profound self-realization at sea is rooted not only in his love for sails and in the art and the tradition of seamanship but also in his fundamental love for work. In "Well Done," while writing about the "successive generations that went out to sea from these [British] Isles," Conrad comments:

> A man is a worker. If he is not that he is nothing. Just nothing — like a mere adventurer. . . . For the great mass of mankind the only saving grace that is needed is steady fidelity to what is nearest to hand and heart in the short moment of each human effort. In other and in greater words, what is needed is a sense of immediate duty, and a feeling of impalpable constraint. (*NLL,* pp. 190–91)

In this passage work, or fidelity to duty, as an end in itself becomes for Conrad the basic salvation of man's existence. Such a view is of crucial importance for this discussion of Conrad's sea fiction, for if Conrad can be so sure that man is a worker, then he can (at least in his period of early sea fiction) avoid some of the metaphysical paralysis troubling those of his contemporaries who believed that man possesses no vision of purposiveness at all. In fact, by consistently portraying characters who continue to work despite the darkness or even the cosmic emptiness surrounding them and who thus, almost as if they are receiving a reward, become conscious of an awakening to a life of individualized purposiveness, Conrad actually makes work (and its justification) the sine qua non of his early sea fiction. In a sense, it is true, such emphasis upon work traps him in a teleological frame that tends to limit the possible directions his sea tales can take, but the ramifications of this problem need not be a concern at this point. Here it is enough to observe the general tenor of purposiveness behind Conrad's use of navigational metaphor.

At the beginning of "Tradition" Conrad writes about work with a particular teleological emphasis:

> "Work is the law. Like iron that lying idle degenerates into a mass of useless rust, like water that in an unruffled pool sickens into a stagnant corrupt state, so without action the spirit of men turns to a dead thing, loses it force, ceases prompting us to leave some trace of ourselves on this earth." The sense of the above lines does not belong to me. It may be found in the note-books of one of the greatest artists that ever lived, Leonardo da Vinci. It has a simplicity and a truth which no amount of subtle comment can destroy. (*NLL*, p. 194)

Here the words of "one of the greatest artists that ever lived" point to another supreme fact behind Conrad's early navigational metaphor: the rise to the stature of navigator, to the status of a sailor who respects and participates in the great tradition of seamanship, is essentially the rise to *the stature of artist*. Such stature is very suggestive, for if one recognizes that the artist is the one individual who is very conscious of ends, or of the purposes of his creations, one can here begin to understand how it is that Conrad invests his early sea fiction with such heroic overtones. Conrad's regard for the genuine sailor not merely as a worker but as an artist may already be self-evident in his appreciation of sailing as a fine art. In *The Mirror of the Sea*, however, Conrad provides a stronger basis for the theme of artistry behind his navigational metaphor when he broadly defines the artist as "a man of action, whether he creates a personality, invents an expedient, or finds the issue of a complicated situation" (*MS*, p. 33). This passage, by broadening artistry to the development of any productive end, allows Conrad (at least potentially) to turn all of his hardworking sailors into artists and thus into heroic navigators. In Conrad's mind the professional sailor, by belonging to a long and rich tradition of seamanship, automatically possesses a solid teleological frame that provides him with special opportunities for self-growth and moral fulfillment and that will thus, if he does not ignore or resist it, assure him of a marvelous life of artistry and understanding. It is no wonder, then, that Conrad turns a sailor of Marlow's hardworking stature into one of the most remarkable heroes of modern British fiction.

The preceding analyses of Conrad's discussion of his own initiations into seamanship and of his principal attitudes toward life at sea illuminate Conrad's early sea fiction in at least four ways. First, these analyses isolate the predominant theme of the period—the theme of conquering moral ambivalence. In contrast to Conrad's first two novels, *Almayer's Folly* and *An Outcast of the Islands*, works that generally lack a standard of conduct against which Almayer's and Willem's declines may be measured, the period of sea fiction always assumes the tradition of seamanship as the standard against which all characters can be judged. Recently, Royal Roussel may have convincingly demonstrated that Nina and Dain's relationship in *Almayer's Folly* serves as a standard for judging the inadequacies of Almayer's life,[10] but one must remember that this standard hardly survives the first novel—witness the collapse of the relationship between Willems and Aïssa in the second. It is only in *The Nigger of the "Narcissus,"* therefore, a novel in which the inadequacies of the crew are set off against the marvelous seamanship of Allistoun and Singleton, that Conrad is finally able to develop new alternatives to the wretched moral ambivalence of a long succession of characters—such as Karain, Jim, Whalley, and others. With that novel, in fact, the use of navigation as the core of his metaphor becomes especially significant precisely because of its teleological implications: seamanship provides Conrad's characters with the opportunity to become genuine artists and heroes.

Second, the analyses develop a larger appreciation of the significance of specific situations. For example, when Marlow in *Heart of Darkness* disregards his six years of sailing in salt seas to and from the Far East and accepts the command of a freshwater steamer; or when Lord Jim, after languishing in an Eastern hospital following an injury upon a sailing ship, takes the berth of first mate on the *Patna*; or when Captain Whalley, under the financial duress of his own making, sells his barque and becomes captain of the *Sofala* — in all three cases it should now be clear that from the beginning of their new "occupations" in steam these characters face the high probability of violating the code of seamanship. Marlow, of course, despite his harrowing introduction to Congo realities, does persevere in his observance of the tradition of the sea. He is perhaps lucky, for Jim and Whalley fail miserably.

Third, these analyses expose the basis for Conrad's extensive use of irony in the early period of sea fiction. Given the consistency of such a metaphor as seamanship, Conrad frequently explores the ironic possibilities inherent in the narrative that develops out of so firmly directed a core. In "Karain" and the three Marlow tales, for example, he introduces a complex narrative situation that on the surface tends to obfuscate the thrust of the tale but that in the light of Conrad's fundamental attitudes toward his life at sea quickly becomes clarified. The narrator of "Karain" may appear inept; or in "Youth" Marlow may appear hopelessly sentimental and nostalgic; or in *Heart of Darkness* Marlow may seem to possess a vision inferior to Kurtz's final insight—but in all three of these tales, the true genius of these narrators who recount past experiences that have developed and affirmed their respect for sea values becomes undeniable in the larger context of Conrad's basic attitudes toward life at sea. Throughout this tightly woven period, but especially from *Lord Jim* to "The End of the Tether," then, the reader must anticipate the possibility of narrative irony even in the smallest detail of the text.

And fourth, these analyses define the nature of the decline in the period of sea fiction following the publication of *Lord Jim*. Once one appreciates *Lord Jim* both as Conrad's most sensitive presentation of the problems inherent in moral ambivalence and as the culmination of his ironic artistry, the nature of the decline from "Typhoon" to "Tether" becomes almost self-evident. For in those works, instead of pushing his exploration of Marlow's perspective to even more extreme tests than he faces in *Heart of Darkness* and *Lord Jim*, Conrad relaxes his concentration and focuses on lesser issues and ironies—especially the irony of the hero having to depend in a world of steam not only upon himself but also upon the machine and thus upon characters of somewhat questionable stature (MacWhirr and Falk). Such irony is important because it brings into question the thrust of Conrad's earlier themes and "solutions" and thus prepares for Conrad's concentration (after 1902) on "social" rather than "individual" themes. While such irony and theme are clearly of lesser importance at least in comparison to the irony in works such as *Heart of Darkness* and *Lord Jim*, they provide, nevertheless, a fitting conclusion to a period that terminates with a work somewhat pessimistically titled "The End of the Tether." In that novel Conrad's emphatic individualism suffers a major setback.

*for Kath*

# 2
# The Nigger of the "Narcissus":
# The New Metaphor

The greatness of *The Nigger of the "Narcissus"* is precisely that it achieves what Conrad set out to do. In the preface, which was originally suppressed, Conrad articulates a now very familiar credo: "My task which I am trying to achieve is, by the power of the written word to make you hear, to make you feel—it is, before all, to make you *see*. That—and no more, and it is everything" (p. xiv). In this novel, with the objectification of the crew's moral ambivalence in the characterization of Wait and Donkin and then in the metaphoric disabling of the *Narcissus* by both the gale and the mutiny, Conrad does allow the reader to see and to hear all the moral ambiguities inherent in the crew's determined pursuit of decency and gentility. This objectification through character and metaphor, a matter I shall take up later, is, however, only half of the success. The other half, because it introduces a basic teleology into Conrad's fiction from 1897 to 1902, is the thorough use of navigational metaphor, particularly as it is associated with Allistoun and Singleton.

By now many critics have observed the details that point to Captain Allistoun's superiority of attitude aboard the *Narcissus*. What they have sometimes missed is how Allistoun fits Conrad's description of the ideal seaman. The fact that Allistoun never leaves the poop during the gale that eventually tips the *Narcissus* on her side is obvious testimony to his stature as captain. The fact, however, that he keeps "his gaze riveted upon [the ship] as a loving man watches the unselfish toil of a delicate woman upon the slender thread of whose existence is hung the whole meaning and joy of the world'' (p. 50), is a more subtle indication that Allistoun appears as the epitome of Conrad's conscientious seaman, the sailor who completely surrenders himself in devotion to his ship. During the crisis of disabling, furthermore, as the superb artist who mediates the struggle between ship and sea,[1] Allistoun also manages to keep his ''gaze fixed ahead, watchful, like a man looking out for a sign'' (p. 62) of potential relief for his ship. He may for a long time seem to see nothing, but at the same time, much in the manner of a hero, he finally appears to the narrator ''to hold the ship up [by himself] in a superhuman concentration of effort'' (p. 65). In all such details Allistoun clearly achieves a heroic stature that is the full measure of Conrad's ideal seaman rooted in the tradition of his craft and that, consequently, makes him deserving of the task of commanding from a poop of ''Olympian heights'' (p. 31).

But Allistoun also knows the limits of his tradition. Toward the beginning of the novel, when Belfast steals the officers' Sunday pie for James Wait's personal enjoyment, all the sailors and the officers seem to anticipate a serious collapse of order and routine. It is a situation about which the narrator urbanely rationalizes: ''Such stealing in a merchant ship is difficult to check, and may be taken as a declaration by men of their dislike for their officers. It is a bad symptom. It may end in God knows what trouble. The *Narcissus* was still a peaceful ship, but mutual confidence was shaken'' (p. 38). The captain, however, does not accept such rationalizing. From past experience he thoroughly understands the precarious nature of preserving discipline on merchant ships. In this situation he may display no extraordinary reaction as he lets the unrest play itself out. Later, after suppressing the more serious threat of mutiny from the crew grumbling over Wait's rights, he may again react rather calmly and tell his first mate, Mr. Baker,

> Queer lot [the crew]. . . . I suppose it's all right now. Can never tell tho', nowadays, with such a . . . Years ago; I was a young master then—one China voyage I had a mutiny; real mutiny, Baker. Different men tho'. . . . We knocked them about for two days, and when they had enough—gentle as lambs. Good crew. And a smart trip I made. (P. 137)

In both instances, however, the captain's cool demeanor, based upon the knowledge of past success under fire, underscores his appreciation of the uncertainty of maintaining discipline aboard a merchant ship. He knows the limits of the tradition and thus the dangers inherent in the service, and with such knowledge he becomes the primary exhibit of seamanship aboard the *Narcissus*.

Indeed, when Allistoun officiates at the *Narcissus*'s resurrection following the gale's abatement—this passage is one of the most moving in all of Conrad's fiction—he displays precisely what one expects of him: a consummate mastery of his art. By shrewdly motivating the mates and the crew to action before they have a chance to retreat into moods of self-pity or of indifference, he reveals his complete understanding of the physical and psychological forces with which he must contend. Even when Donkin refuses to do his share, he easily assumes the demeanor appropriate to the occasion: "I will brain you with this belaying pin if you don't catch hold of the brace" (p. 86). Allistoun knows what faithful devotion to his ship requires, and despite the easy discipline of the merchant marine, he does not back off from the extreme necessities of the moment. The sailors themselves, in turn, become fully aware of the force of his character—especially when, exhausted, they plead for rest from the exacting demands of his orders. Mr. Baker may be the man who in that context fiercely denounces them, "No! No rest till the work is done," but throughout the scene it is evident that the sailors' acceptance of the mate's challenging remarks is essentially rooted in their respect for the captain's own firm determination to get the job done before the men retire to their bunks. On the occasion of the *Narcissus*'s resurrection, therefore, Allistoun virtually by the strength of his own character raises the ship from her submerging. Throughout the voyage he may have for the most part remained "one of those commanders who speak little, seem to hear nothing, look at no one — and [yet who] know everything, hear every whisper, see every fleeting shadow of their ship's life" (p. 125). He has found, nevertheless, a "taciturn serenity in the profound depths of a larger experience," and thus he never displays—even later in the uneasy moment of confining the demoralizing Wait to his cabin (an act that some critics have disparaged)—the enervating weakness of moral hesitation that may attend such heightened self-awareness, no matter how mature. Allistoun is unquestionably the principal force of seamanship in the tale.

Singleton displays a similar force of character. Like Allistoun's, his primary attitude at sea is devotion to his ship and to his craft. Indeed, because he has spent so little time (no more than forty months) on land during his long career at sea, one might also conclude that devotion to ship and craft also characterizes his experience on land. Already by the end of the first chapter, therefore, shortly before he performs the novel's first act of seamanship (he tightens the anchor brake), Singleton achieves a very symbolic stature that thoroughly conditions the reader's response to his character for the remainder of the novel. At that point, standing in the darkened doorway of the forecastle, his face to the light, he appears as "old as Father Time himself" or as a major representative of Conrad's great tradition:

> [Singleton's] generation lived inarticulate and indispensable, without knowing the sweetness of affections or the refuge of a home—and died free from the dark menace of a narrow grave. They were the everlasting children of the mysterious sea. Their successors [including the present crew of the *Narcissus*] are the grown-up children of a discontented earth. They are less naughty, but less innocent; less profane, but perhaps also less believing; and if they have learned how to speak they have also learned how to whine. But the others were strong and mute; they were effaced, bowed and enduring, like stone caryatides that hold up in the night the lighted halls of a resplendent and glorious edifice. They are gone now—and it does not matter. (P. 25)

Here Singleton, like the Conrad who regards himself as a "bizarre relic" of a tradition that has turned into a "monstrous antiquity,"[2] becomes a full representative of the old art and the old traditions, which at that time were already giving way to modern steamships and their timetables. The *Narcissus*, to be sure, is a sailing vessel, and on the surface it would appear that in her service the old art and traditions must prevail. In fact, however, Singleton alone (at least of the crew) is a sailor in the best sense of the tradition. His is an isolation that effectively prevents him from becoming actively involved with his more selfish mates.

On occasion, Singleton does speak to his fellows on matters other than of professional concern, but on those occasions his opinions merely shock and distress the crew. When the sailors relentlessly fondle Wait, for example, Singleton quietly remonstrates with the black and, by implication, with his mates: "Well, get on with your dying" (p. 42). The implication of the remark is not so much that Singleton wants Wait to die but that he wants the affairs of the ship to return to that professional basis which he has learned to respect from his participation in the heyday of sailing as an art. Later, during the initial stages of mutiny, when Donkin is trying to enlist the men in Wait's support, Singleton again quietly but firmly warns the men, "You can't help [Wait]; die he must" (p. 130). Here Singleton once more calls the men back to their duty. In both instances, however, Singleton's bold words strike the men only as "incomprehensible and exciting, like an oracle behind a veil." Because the sailors are so enmeshed in their own pursuits of decency (the veil actually covers their own eyes), they generally ignore Singleton's counsel and remain blind to the implication of being called back to the performance of their craft. Toward the end of the voyage, when Singleton in reaction to Wait's dying finally begins to rely upon what passes for superstition but what is really only a mystical reflection of his long experience, the crew may possess some justification for such complete disregard. After all, who can believe, as Singleton does, that Wait will die in sight of land and that the becalmed *Narcissus* will upon that death receive a fair breeze? Singleton proves to be correct, however, and at that point the fact that his voice serves as the oracle of the ship and thus as testimony not to his ability in superstition but to his wonderful understanding of his craftsmanship entirely escapes his more modern peers.

That Singleton is such a wonderful sailor is apparent not only in his symbolic stature as representative of the old tradition and in his oracular insight but also in his self-discipline at the wheel during the thirty hours of the *Narcissus*'s disabling. At the wheel Singleton may confront the naked elements in all their fury, but there he also remains firm in strength and in devotion to his art: "His hair flew out in the wind; the gale seemed to take its life-long adversary by the beard and shake his old head. He wouldn't let go, and, with his knees forced between the spokes, flew up and down like a man on a bough" (p. 60). Singleton does take a beating, but when Allistoun prepares to raise the *Narcissus* to even keel, he is the crew member who is most ready for the challenge. In this instance Allistoun may function as the prime mover; Singleton, nevertheless, serves at least as the helmsman—the "Single" to the "All"—whose action becomes the basis for the captain's success. As helmsman, in fact, Singleton possesses a wonderful opportunity to reveal himself as a thorough professional and as an artist; he does not waste the chance: "In front of his erect figure only the two arms moved crosswise with a swift and sudden readiness, to check or urge again the rapid stir of circling spokes. He steered with care" (p. 89). The care alone underscores the fact that this old man understands the craft that the younger, modern sailors frequently neglect in Conrad's early sea fiction.

It is true, to be sure, that this attention to craft also exhausts the old Singleton. When he returns to the forecastle following his long turn at the wheel, for example, he "crash[es] down, stiff and headlong like an uprooted tree" (p. 97). In that moment, and for the first time in his life, he probably even comprehends (as the narrator suggests) the significance of time—both the personal fact of growing old and, perhaps, the larger fact of the gradual uprooting of his tradition. Certainly he now understands the sea as "an immensity tormented and blind, moaning and furious, that claimed all the days of his tenacious life, and, when life was over, would claim the worn-out body of its slave" (p. 99). At midnight, however, when his watch is called—and much to the surprise of the younger, less devoted sailors who expect him to be forever "broken" by the gale—he appears on deck "as if nothing had been the matter" (p. 98). In truth, nothing is. For while Singleton may now be painfully conscious of death's inevitability, whether in relation to himself or to the tradition of his youth, he is still ready in his exhaustion to demonstrate that seamanship which has in the past made of him a man. The problem in the novel lies, therefore, not in Allistoun and Singleton, men cut from the same cloth, but in the younger sailors who display the effects of modern attitudes and who, instead of loving the sea, are primarily interested in establishing a comfortable position for themselves on land. It is necessary, now, to turn to the narrator's analysis of this crew, especially his objectification of their attitudes through characterization and metaphor, in order to demonstrate the full extent of the genius within Allistoun and Singleton.

There are moments when the narrator does appreciate the mettle of the *Narcissus*'s sailors. He knows, for example, that the roll call the night before the *Narcissus* sails from Bombay is a "call to unquiet loneliness, to inglorious and obscure struggle" (p.15), and thus while he may through the greater part of his narrative disparage, if only by implication, the characters and deeds of his mates, he also — having himself matured in the *Narcissus* experience — genuinely shares the significance of Conrad's appreciation of

the true peace of God [which] begins at any spot a thousand miles from the nearest land; . . . when He sends there the messengers of

His might it is not in terrible wrath against crime, presumption, and folly, but paternally, to chasten simple hearts — ignorant hearts that know nothing of life, and beat undisturbed by envy or greed. (P. 31)

On the *Narcissus* the men know the brotherhood not only of mere vocation but also of chastening. During the harsh gales off the Cape, for example, they display a seamanship of which Conrad himself might have been proud. There they recognize that the *Narcissus* possesses a weakness that makes her conduct rather unpredictable and even cranky, but in that context, instead of bemoaning their association with such a ship, they begin to regard the *Narcissus* as "the most magnificent sea boat ever launched." On her, they realize, they can display their own capacities for devotion and service, and thus when the captain engineers the ship's hard progress through the strong winds, they warmly applaud his efforts to help his ship: "Our hearts went out to the old man when he pressed her hard so as to make her hold her own" (p. 51). The result of such response is that they become "a ready group [awaiting] the first sharp order of an officer." Once the storm arrives, of course, there is a rapid succession of orders. Before the *Narcissus* topples to her side the men "with immense efforts" and "through a merciless buffeting" (p. 55) furl the topsails; a few hours later, "in attitudes of crucifixion," they goosewing the main topsail; and finally, even though exhausted by the thirty-six hours of disabling, they again obey Allistoun's orders and thus reveal their mettle. For such performance Mr. Baker regards them as "a good crowd, . . . [at least] as they go nowadays" (p. 103).

The captain, however, especially following Donkin's tossing of the belaying-pin, knows that he "could count the real sailors amongst [the crew] on the fingers of one hand" (p. 126). Despite the crew's sometime display of real seamanship, their hearts are for the most part prey not to the true peace of God but to feelings of envy and greed. Much in the fashion of Almayer and Willems, the principals in Conrad's first two novels, in fact, the crew of the *Narcissus* are thoroughly bent only upon establishing their character of superiority or of gentility during the ship's return voyage from Bombay to London. Already before the initial muster of the men, when Donkin stands before them a "sympathetic and deserving" beggar without clothes, the sailors immediately extend to him their extra clothing and congratulate themselves upon their easy compassion and benevolence. Then, shortly after the voyage begins, some of them engage in a heated conversation concerning "the characteristics of a gentleman" (p. 32) — whether gentility requires money, a manner of speaking, or clothes. At that point, while asserting their individual viewpoints, the sailors suddenly find themselves involved in a whole series of strange and ridiculous arguments, and yet, instead of recognizing the almost inescapable irony of their arguing angrily over the nature of gentility, they actually persist in their divisiveness of feeling. Obviously, no matter what follies attend their behavior, they do not want to relinquish their cherished dreams.

From the beginning of the novel, then, the narrator is aware of the crew's moral ambivalence. Such awareness, in fact, provides much of the focus for his narrative, for it is this awareness that underlies his ambiguous characterizations of James Wait and Donkin as virtual epitomes of modern sailors who are interested not in their craft but in their own comfort and prerogatives. The sick Wait, for example, as a "black man sitting apart in a meditative attitude and as motionless as a carving" (p. 45), already achieves near the beginning of the voyage the questionable status of the sacred. In his own mind he is not sick, and yet by the time the *Narcissus* reaches the Atlantic, he has managed to make his sick-cabin (at least in the brilliance of moonlight) the "silver shrine [of] a black idol" (p. 105). By playing upon his supposed (yet very real) illness he has made himself appear the worthy object of appreciation and devotion and has even succeeded in tyrannizing the genteel sailors who wish to be decent toward him. At the same time, however, when his mates serve him in bed, they become conscious of themselves as the "base courtiers of a hated prince" who regards them with "unconciliating criticism" (p. 37). Or they become aware of Wait as the origin of the "infernal spell" (p. 37), then the "weird servitude" (p. 43), and finally the something "worse than a nightmare" (p. 44), in which they increasingly find themselves trapped. By that point illness has blurred with the sacred, devotion with servitude. Everything has become so ambiguous that the sailors, while dealing with a Wait who may or may not be shamming illness but who is obviously taking advantage of them, know only the extremes of infernal worship or bitter self-contempt. In their consternation, of course, they do not recognize that the ambiguities that surround Wait are ultimately projections of their own lack of integrity as sailors who should belong by vocation to a well-defined tradition.

Similarly, yet in reverse, Donkin from the beginning of the voyage becomes the object not of the crew's compassion but of their contempt. Because he lacks the quiet Wait's "secret of keeping for ever on the run the fundamental imbecility of mankind" (p. 37), the loquacious Donkin asserts his rights but generally finds himself left alone or in the untenable position of cringing before the crew. In the first half of the novel, in fact, whenever he displays his ready insolence to the officers, he finds himself immediately isolated — morally — from the rest of the crew. For example, in response to his cry that the spars of the disabled *Narcissus* must be cut, one of the sailors strikes him with a "back-handed blow over the mouth" (p. 60). Or when he angrily encourages the weary sailors to hit Mr. Baker for badgering Jack Knowles during the ship's disabling, several of the sailors threaten to hit him if he does not keep quiet. Following the *Narcissus*'s recovery and the crew's return to good spirits, nevertheless, this beggar suddenly begins to impress the men with his counsel. At that point, having recently endured more suffering than they think should be the lot of the genteel, the sailors again, as before Wait, become conscious of a very ambiguous response of extremes: "Our contempt for him was unbounded — and we could not but listen with interest to that consummate artist" (p. 100). To be sure, it may only be their weariness that now makes these sailors very susceptible to Donkin's undiminishing chatter concerning their rights and the basic equality of their manhood to that of the officers. They, however, have throughout the voyage devoted themselves to the pursuit of gentility, and thus now, even though it is much to their dismay, they actually discover themselves reduced to the *necessity* of accepting this beggar as the champion, if not the idol, of their cause. Although they will never openly admit it, he becomes the "man"[3] for having stood up for their rights while they merely cringed in the manner, as Donkin several times pointedly suggests, of "a driven lot of sheep" (p. 110).

In both these situations, Wait as object of devotion and as origin of servitude, and Donkin as beggar and as man, the crew's own moral ambivalence, or their lack of allegiance to the tradition of seamanship, is the real issue. With the arrival of the gale off the Cape this fact takes on an even darker character. For now, instead of trying to determine the subtle issue of whether or not Wait is shamming his illness, or of whether or not Donkin's chatter concerning his rights contains any merit, the men face a world of "shattered creation" in which "nothing seems left . . . but darkness, clamour, fury — and the ship" (p. 54). As men who lack moral focus and who generally labor under the paralysis of moral ambiguities, these sailors find themselves quite unable to deal effectively with the circumstances before them. Ironically, much as it is for Lord Jim, it is as if their earlier ambition to achieve a genteel, per-

haps heroic stature now precludes their rising to the challenges of seamanship inherent in the disabling. Indeed, when the matured narrator
later remembers how some of them, instead of focusing upon the
primary matter of preserving the ship, want to cut off the ship's masts in
order to restore balance to her keel, he is surely exposing them as men
who — like Wait and Donkin — have only their selfish interests at heart
and who, therefore, under the terrific force of the gale deserve their
reduction to cold and mute corpses for having failed to live up to the
traditions of their craft. Unquestionably, he expends a good deal of effort describing the "dark patches under the eyes," the "hollows of
sunken cheeks," and the lips "livid and thin" (p. 74) — all of which
suggest not merely the crew's degeneration into physical stupor but also
their complete psychic surrender to the moral collapse of which the
*Narcissus*'s disabling is itself a further metaphor.

To be sure, these sailors do act — and bravely, they think — when
they rescue Donkin from falling overboard and Wait from being sub-
merged in his coffinlike cabin. These rescues, too, however, merely
confirm the sailors in their foolish pursuit of gentility. For once the gale
has subsided and the *Narcissus* is again making way and the men have a
chance to recover from their weariness of body and mind, they immediately begin to consider whether they possess an obligation to justify and
enhance their wonderful deeds of rescue. Having at least rescued Donkin and Wait from death, they now find it easy to forget their despair
and general stupor during the gale and to boast, instead, of their
"pluck" and "energy": "We remembered honourable episodes: our
devotion, our indomitable perseverance — and were proud of them as
though they had been the outcome of our unaided impulses" (p. 100).
The upshot is that the men actually intensify their support of the two
men on board the ship who least deserve it. Such a rationalization of
their conduct during the gale is terribly ironic. To the matured narrator,
who himself participated in the rescue of Wait, the rationalizing is probably also a galling memory. With his more experienced perspective he
now knows that such rationalization, such determined justification of
past decencies, is completely unwarranted and even dangerous because
it pushes the crew closer to the brink of mutiny. He knows that once the
self-deceiving crew have firmly identified themselves with both Wait
and Donkin by virtue of the recent rescues (to this point they have
avoided such full identification because of their ambivalencies), they

have become embroiled in a web of relationships that can bode, for them and for the ship, nothing but ill.

Instead of dealing summarily with the bickering Donkin, the crew now seem to submerge what little remains of their negligible respect for the tradition of seamanship in their identification with Donkin: Donkin's "care for our rights, his disinterested concern for our dignity, were not discouraged by the invariable contumely of our words, by the disdain of our looks" (p. 100). Here, then, if only by virtue of the crew's silence and lack of expression, Donkin, the champion of the heroes' rights, finally gains his opportunity for a full offensive against the officers. The immediate occasion for the attempt is Captain Allistoun's firm sequestering of the shamming and demoralizing Wait. For Donkin, of course, now that the sailors have firmly identified themselves with both Donkin and Wait, it is the ideal occasion, and thus he fires his arguments to an intensity that he expects the sailors not to withstand: (1) Wait, the idol, the sailors' possession by virtue of the rescue, must not be deprived of his right to fresh air; (2) the crew, men as much as their officers, deserve self-determination. The sailors, nevertheless, with a lingering respect for the real tradition of heroism at sea still intact, only anticipate a weak possibility for transforming the ship's order. They know that they want a better life, preferably the leisurely life of the genteel on land, but at the same time (and somewhat surprisingly) they possess enough allegiance to the traditions of the sea not to be swayed entirely by Donkin's arguments. When Donkin tosses the belaying-pin, therefore, his action does not enflame the crew to the full passion of mutiny. Instead, he hears Archie's sudden shout, "If you do oot ageen I wull tell!" And there are also shouts from others: "'Don't!' — 'Drop it!' — 'We aint that kind!'" (p. 123). Perhaps it is only the abruptness and the extremity of Donkin's action that awaken the crew to renewed respect for the order that long experience in sails cannot avoid teaching, but they do awaken. In fact, when the *Narcissus* in the heat of Donkin's passion suddenly swerves off course (a maneuver that serves as another metaphor for the crew's imminent moral collapse), the crew immediately and willingly heed Allistoun's orders and bring the ship back to course.

The awakening and then the ready observance of the captain's orders, however, do not argue a transformation of attitude in the crew. Several of them spend a night of fruitless talk generating enthusiasm about the present crisis, and the next morning most of them still anticipate some redress of their grievances, if not the announcement of the second coming. The captain, fully conscious of the mounting discontent and resentment and especially of Donkin's instigations, is ready for the muster and blisters the men with a scathing denunciation that gradually brings them to their senses: "Tell you what's the matter? Too big for your boots. Think yourselves damn good men. Know half your work. Do half your duty. Think it too much. If you did ten times as much it wouldn't be enough" (p. 134). In summary fashion he defuses the mutiny by exposing the crew's inadequacies as men — surely an ironic development in view of their desire to become genteel. Then, ordering Donkin to return the belaying-pin to its proper place, he displays the soundness of his authority over the ship. Immediately the crew lose their tolerance for the humiliated Donkin. Even after this confirmation of a lingering allegiance to seamanship during the mutiny, however, they remain basically unchanged, for they continue to be very much interested in their decent treatment of Wait. Their characters, consequently, seem very ambiguous, at times positive, then again negative, but that very ambiguity is full testimony to the fact that they have not been able to get off the rollers of moral ambivalence.

Generally, then, on this voyage from Bombay to London the sailors of the *Narcissus* learn nothing. Even during the last stages of the voyage, when they should be fully aware of the deceptive quality of appearances, they continue to humor the dying Wait and, blinded by their sympathy, to ignore the real question underlying Wait's conduct — whether or not he is shamming. In such a situation it is obvious that these sailors are essentially humoring only themselves, or more to the point, their conception of themselves. For just as Wait — the idol who already during his rescue is only a "bladder full of gas" (p. 70) or a "cold black skin loosely stuffed with soft cotton wool" (p. 71) or a "doll that had lost half its sawdust" (p. 72) or an "old bolster" (p. 73) — foolishly ignores the ultimate discovery that "all his [physical and moral] inside was gone" (p. 113), or just as Donkin — reduced in James Wait's presence to nothing more than a "screechin' poll-parrot" or a "dirty white cockatoo" (p. 110) and later to a vulture who "seemed busy gnawing his way through [his chest] as if to get at the heart within" (p. 132) — consistently ignores the gross ineffectuality of his bickering, so the sailors themselves, corpses during the gale and less than men during the mutiny, ignore the scathing criticism of their captain and rather quickly return to the comfortable pursuit of narcissistic definition as decent and genteel. Toward the end of the voyage the decadence of the sailors' self-deception becomes inescapable:

> Through [Wait] we were becoming highly humanized, tender, complex, excessively decadent; we understood the subtlety of his fear, sympathized with all his repulsions, shrinkings, evasions, delusions—as though we had been overcivilized, and rotten, and without any knowledge of the meaning of life. We had the air of being initiated in some infamous mysteries. . . . We were inexpressibly vile and very much pleased with ourselves. (P. 139)

It is in this sense of extreme self-deception, of course, that Wait and Donkin chiefly serve as the objectification of the moral confusion in the entire crew.

That such confusion lingers even at the end of this voyage home is especially evident in the fact that upon Wait's death, the sailors suddenly confront "the death of an old belief"—the belief that they understand Wait's shamming. This death provides the catastrophe: "A common bond was gone; the strong, effective and respectable bond of a sentimental lie" (p. 155). Without this belief the sailors face the dilemma of surrendering all illusion of recent moral purpose. And thus, in order to avoid such a drastic necessity, they immediately begin, rather stupidly, to engage in a "violent quarrelling as to the exact moment of Jimmy's death" (p. 157)—with the intention of verifying whether that moment had coincided with the fall in the barometer and thus with Singleton's belief in the promise of a breeze for the becalmed *Narcissus* upon Wait's death. With this new pursuit of a verification that is impossible but that may supplant their previous "sentimental lie," these sailors unmistakably remain the fools, the figures of moral ambivalence, who have answered the first muster on the ship. The narrator, singularly unobtrusive but obviously appreciative of Allistoun and Singleton and thus skeptical of his shipmates' activities, is the one possible exception to this pattern of folly—during the voyage he may have matured.

In the light of past criticism on the novel, which has frequently argued that during the *Narcissus*'s homeward voyage the crew move toward insight and even self-realization, the present discussion of the crew's pursuit of gentility, as a land concern completely outside the scope of the seaman's tradition, becomes the crucial matter of the novel. For once one is aware of these sailors as the originators of a moral farce that is essentially extraneous to their daily occupations, it is possible to recognize them as characters in Conrad's fictional world who must be responsible for whatever misery they experience. Furthermore, because they have separated themselves from a viable tradition pregnant with opportunity for self-realization, it is even possible to define them as some of Conrad's greatest fools. These points may now seem—after lengthy discussion in this chapter—rather obvious, but if referred to the context of Conrad's first three long works the significance of these points becomes crucial.

One must remember that the sailors of the *Narcissus* do perceive themselves as a "community of banded criminals" (p. 156) late in the voyage. In his first three long works, *Almayer's Folly, An Outcast of the Islands,* and "The Return," Conrad explores what many critics have regarded as the fin de siècle paralysis of moral ambivalence.[4] The Almayer and Willems who are conscious of a moral and racial superiority within the terrible isolation of Sambir, the Lingard who exults in controlling Sambir and dreams of amassing a fortune in gold, the Hervey who becomes the victim of a middle-class idealism concerning love when he discovers his wife's indifference—all four men find themselves trapped in circumstances that allow for little self-realization. Lingard may seem to enjoy some moral fulfillment in his "pirating" of Far Eastern seas or in his virtual governing of Sambir, but when Willems betrays him into the hands of the Arab, he simply disappears from the scene of his disillusionment and forever disappoints the Almayer who is depending on Lingard's proffer of wealth. The four principals in these three early works, therefore, never know the grace of moral development. They may perceive their unhappiness, but they never understand that they themselves are the agents of their dissatisfactions. Unlike the crew of the *Narcissus*, who must finally face up to the lie (and its implications), these four men too often blame others or external circumstances for what has gone wrong in their lives. Witness, here, Lingard's increasing hate of Willems even though he suspects that he himself is largely responsible for having created the circumstances that ultimately lead to Willems's complete disorientation. The crew of the *Narcissus*, on the other hand, probably because they can never entirely escape the sailing traditions that even after the heyday of sails continue to judge the quality of their moral conduct, must—on occasion at least—shoulder full responsibility for their follies and misdeeds. The standards of seamanship, therefore, sharply distinguish their lives from Conrad's earlier protagonists' by providing them with the possibility of a moral watershed or of heightened moral sensibility.

In a recent book Royal Roussel has shrewdly pointed out that already in *Almayer's Folly* Conrad has faced up to the necessity of defining a standard for human conduct. He begins by citing the fact that when Nina returns to Sambir following her education in Singapore, she finds the basis for all moral perspectives inadequate; having been educated among white Protestants, but now surrounded by several factions of a jungle community, she observes "the narrow mantle of civilized morality . . . fall away and leave her shivering and helpless as if on the edge of some deep and unknown abyss" (p. 42). For her, in fact, as for Almayer and Willems, Sambir quickly becomes a world of "outer darkness" (p. 16) and of "appalling blackness" (p. 19). And yet, even though she is overwhelmed by this new world, she retains enough of the Protestant ethic to despise the aimlessness of her Sambir life: "It seemed so unreasonable, so humiliating . . . to see the days rush by into the past, without a hope, a desire, or an aim that would justify the life she had to endure in ever-growing weariness" (p. 151). Such bitterness, of course, encourages her to respond to the passion of Dain Maroola, the prince whose active and confident demeanor serves as an obvious contrast to the ineffectuality of Almayer and to the bickering of the leaders of Sambir, and eventually such a response leads her from her moral paralysis to rebirth and fulfillment: "She recognized with a thrill of delicious fear the mysterious consciousness of her identity with that being. Listening to his words, it seemed to her she was born only then to a knowledge of a new existence, that her life was complete only when near him, and she abandoned herself to a feeling of dreamy happiness" (p. 64). That passion can function here as a viable ethic is probably also apparent in the acknowledgment at the end of the narrative that Nina and Dain have enjoyed the birth of a son, a new heir to perpetuate the kingdom. Roussel's argument, with which I agree, is that Conrad tempers Almayer's moral confusion with the passionate relationship between Nina and Dain.[5]

The fact that *Almayer's Folly* ends with a solution of passion suggests that Conrad began his writing career with some teleology in mind. This teleology may have failed Conrad as he gradually became more absorbed in the question of what constitutes a viable standard of conduct (witness Willems's failure in *An Outcast of the Islands*), but the resolution of the first novel still defines a fundamental optimism in the author's point of view that probably prompted him, finally, to adopt navigational metaphor as a standard for conduct in *The Nigger of the "Narcissus."* Some critics, to be sure, have already recognized a fundamental optimism of viewpoint in the narrative of the book. Too often, however, this optimism is merely a function of their mistaken belief that during the *Narcissus*'s homeward journey the crew "passes from ignorance to knowledge about life and about death."[6] If there is a basic narrative optimism in the novel, that optimism must center upon the possibilities in a seaman such as the narrator himself for living up to the demands of the traditions in which Allistoun and Singleton are rooted. Critics may continue to argue that the essential problem before the sailors of the *Narcissus* is merely that "they do not know for sure whether [Wait] is sick or not"[7] or that they are overwhelmed by the consciousness of "the limiting conditions of life."[8] Such arguments, however, as long as they disregard the careful contrast around which Conrad has organized the novel, will always prove insufficient—and sometimes even dead wrong. Allistoun and Singleton are the heroic ideals, the standards by which all seamen can organize their conduct, and their very existence as men becomes the guarantee of the possibility in Conrad's early fiction for growth or maturation, for development of perspective. The sailors of the *Narcissus* fail to achieve such growth even though they succeed in bringing the ship home, but the fact that such achievement is possible or that there are ends and purposes to man's existence is, perhaps, optimism enough in a fictional world so generally characterized by the somber hues of darkness and decay.

# 3

# Narrative Irony in "Karain: A Memory"

Once one appreciates the tension in *The Nigger of the "Narcissus"* between the style of Allistoun and Singleton and that of the crew, one can hypothesize that at least the narrator, as one member of the crew, has enjoyed a development of insight during the voyage from Bombay to London. Indeed, if it is remembered that the narrator, as one of the three rescuers who break through the bulkhead in order to reach the trapped James Wait during the *Narcissus*'s disabling, has himself thoroughly participated in the crew's decent treatment of Wait,[1] or that throughout the voyage he has had abundant opportunity to become involved in the crew's confusion over whether or not Wait is sick and then over whether or not to mutiny in support of his rights, one can develop a fairly solid basis for defining the nature of his new insight. By the time the crew experiences its moral collapse upon Wait's death, this narrator has begun to understand the folly of the crew's pursuit of gentility and to realize a need for separating himself entirely from their interests and preoccupations. While his mates argue about whether Wait's death coincides with the fall in the barometer, therefore, he (as the shift in narrative person from third to first underscores)[2] increasingly sides himself with the viewpoint of Allistoun and Singleton and then during the final leg of the voyage takes care to maintain such separation from the crew. Witness here the very end of the voyage when the narrator, instead of joining his mates for a bit of camaraderie and the fostering of the "illusions of

47

strength, mirth, happiness'' (p. 171), goes his own way. Although having for a time participated in the crew's follies, this singularly unobtrusive narrator has in fact learned much about the significance of the craft during the long and arduous voyage of the *Narcissus* from Bombay. In London, consequently, he accepts for himself the lonely but mature stature of craftsmanship that such learning entails.

This change in stature, in addition to providing the impetus for narrating the tale, provides the narrator with an essentially ironic point of view. For while he is conscious of a ''rebirth'' in the disabled *Narcissus* and eventually of a transformation in himself, he knows that the crew's supposed rebirth is hardly real. With the disabled *Narcissus*'s rise the crew may be conscious of a rebirth—it was ''as though we had died and had been resuscitated'' (p. 100)—but by the end of the voyage, and certainly upon further reflection, the narrator himself knows that these crew members have never belonged to the craft of seamanship (at least not in the manner of Singleton) and thus will probably never know rebirth while at sea. At the very end of the novel, in a forgiving mood of nostalgia, he may evoke the crew of the *Narcissus*: ''Haven't we together and upon the immortal sea, wrung out a meaning from our sinful lives? Good-bye, brothers! You were a good crowd'' (p. 173). Such a soft comment, however, should not deceive the reader. The narrator's judgment, based upon his appreciation of Allistoun and Singleton, is sure: the crew with their determined pursuit of decency and gentility have actually embroiled themselves in land considerations that in the context of the hard life at sea can only awaken in them the turmoils of moral ambivalence. No matter how emphatically critics may stress their rebirth, therefore, the crew's supposed growth of insight remains thoroughly ironic. The sailors of the *Narcissus* are in transit, moving outside the traditions by which Conrad's true heroes in the early sea fiction have organized their lives, and as such figures who ignore the more salient characteristics of genuine seamanship, they enjoy neither the narrator's nor Conrad's pity. In his own response to this crew, the reader does well to follow such a narrative lead.

Conrad's complex handling of narrative in *The Nigger of the ''Narcissus,''* however, remains somewhat hesitant—probably because the character of the narrator even at the end is so shadowy. And yet, while it is not until the later successes with the mature Marlow that Conrad achieves full narrative control, *The Nigger* still serves as an important key for understanding his experiment with narrative in ''Karain'' and eventually in the Marlow tales. From even a quick reading it is clear that the narration of "Karain" in method, if not entirely in theme, largely reflects the manner of the unobtrusive narrator of *The Nigger*. In fact, because the narrator of "Karain" does retain so much of his precursor's aloofness, the crucial question facing the reader in responding to this story, as in responding to *The Nigger,* is the location of vision within its ironic texture. Such a question again necessarily directs one toward a close appraisal of the subtleties by which the narrator manipulates his narrative, but in this case—largely because Conrad is already more accomplished—the appraisal leads to rather full and provocative conclusions concerning the character of the narrator himself.

Such an appraisal, as a result, promises significant improvements in interpretation over previous thematic discussions[3] of the tale, for if it is possible to fix the character of the narrator, it may even be possible to define the nature and the extent of his narrative unreliability. That definition would, in turn, provide an important bridge between the hesitancy of *The Nigger* and Conrad's mature use of the subtle Marlow as the subsequent narrative voice in his early sea fiction. Before I explore the narrator's character and manner, however, I would like to consider for a moment Karain's dilemma in the story. That dilemma, after all, occasions the narrator's interest and provides the basis for his shrewd and discriminating ironies.

Karain, following the betrayal of his friend Matara, initially seems to possess ample opportunity for achieving new moral and philosophic depth. After deliberately killing Matara, for example, he walks "upon a broad path under a clear starlight; and that strange country seemed so big, the rice-fields so vast, that, as [he] looked around, [his] head swam with the fear of space" (p. 39). Such an enlargement of spatial (and sometimes temporal) perspective usually entails for Conrad's real heroes—the Marlows of "Youth" and *Heart of Darkness*, for instance—a maturation of vision or profound self-realization. Karain, however, even in this spatial nightmare, essentially remains conscious only of Matara's ghost. For him, consequently, the frequently illuminating Conradian journey at sea or in the wilderness turns into a determined retreat from the responsibilities of consciously and deliberately navigating Marlow's deaf and dumb universe[4]—or his own universe of "tangled forest, . . . where crumbling old walls had fallen amongst the trees, and where strange stone idols . . . seemed to live and threaten in the light of their camp fire" (p. 32). Eventually in this long flight from

Matara's ghost, Karain even retreats behind the soothing presence of an old sorcerer; and while he there recovers a semblance of his former self-confidence, by then it is clear that his flight-retreat functions as the absolute reverse of Marlow's experience in *Heart of Darkness*. Marlow, while perceiving the terrible emptiness of the Congo wilderness, also recognizes the necessity of creating his own fictions and illusions amid such emptiness and thus finally becomes conscious of profound moral realization. On the surface, at least, Karain may for a time enjoy the possibility of similar growth, but by turning his experience within a wilderness of ghosts into an unilluminating retreat, he destroys that possibility and makes of himself a pathetic figure.

Even then, nevertheless, it is also true that the Karain who leads the Bugis has some years later become the master of a foothold that is shaped "like a young moon" (p. 4) and that is surrounded by a "purple semicircle of hills" (p. 7), and that he himself is surrounded by a "spiked halo of his followers' iron points" or by the fringe of a "red umbrella" (p. 10). Because these circle images suggest a perfection or completion in Karain's life that is mirrored in the narrator's comment that "Karain's quality [is] to appear in the illusion of unavoidable success" (p. 7), it is not surprising that a few readers have concluded that Karain has genuinely achieved on his journeys a moral stature of some proportion. And yet if one follows the narrator's commentary closely, one must recognize that the older Karain's posture as master and leader is never entirely convincing. Even in his first visit as a young seaman to Karain's settlement, the narrator himself, conscious that the community possesses a life "unaccountably empty of anything that would stir the thought, touch the heart, give a hint of the ominous sequence of days" (p. 5), begins to speculate upon "what depth of horrible void" (p. 6) underlies all of Karain's conduct. Eventually, in fact, he finds himself regarding Karain "as an actor, as a human being aggressively disguised." Thereafter, having become conscious of Karain's stature as somewhat questionable, perhaps even fraudulent, he continues to observe (especially years later when he indulges in a rehearsal of that period of his young manhood) how Karain, in order to disguise the restlessness of his spirit, devotes himself to a rigorous stage performance each day of his life. When the sorcerer dies and Karain is without his customary assistance, therefore, the narrator alone fully appreciates the horror in the fact that Karain once more faces the necessity of confronting the wilderness and its ghosts without the defenses of charms and charades. Upon the sorcerer's death Karain, as in the immediate aftermath of Matara's death, may seem to possess an opportunity in which to become (at least if he acknowledges the moral emptiness within the wilderness) the "navigator" of his own experience. In actuality, however, as the narrator realizes, the quality of his moral experience has by then been established, and thus when he swims to the company of the narrator and his fellow sailors and with their assistance hopes to recover his stature as wonderful leader, one must anticipate in the narrative a terrible irony that reflects all the dark ambiguity in the early Conrad.

Most readers of "Karain" have, of course, already recognized that Karain is not one of Conrad's characters of privileged insight. When they have looked for other candidates of vision in the story, however, they have generally generated only further disagreement concerning where, or even whether, such insight exists in the tale. One critic, for example, after briefly concentrating with acumen upon the similarities between the circumstances of Karain and Lord Jim, has merely ignored the ending of the tale (where one might expect some crystallization of vision) as a "trivial anecdote."[5] Another critic has at one point made the young Hollis the giant of vision because it is Hollis who, much like Stein with Lord Jim, marvelously attends to Karain's needs;[6] at another point he has suggested that it is the narrator who is (as a proto-Marlow) "beginning to see the community and the parity of illusion"[7] and who thus becomes the hero of the tale. Because of such critical uncertainty the whole problem of who possesses the supreme vision in the tale actually begs for reexamination. Here, consequently, assuming for the moment that—like *The Nigger of the "Narcissus"*—this tale does contain a character of special insight and that the identity of this character probably becomes most clear in the long scene between Karain and the sailors, I wish to focus the heart of my remaining discussion on the narrator's handling of that scene. I have just noted how, as a young man smuggling guns, this narrator has enjoyed an insight into Karain's dramatizations. Given that fact, as well as the presence of his precursor in *The Nigger*, it seems likely that he will serve as the character of principal vision.

Throughout the tale, as the narrator discusses his own involvement some years earlier in Karain's affairs, he adopts a self-deprecatory tone that is initially very misleading. Near the middle of the tale, for example, shortly before Karain presents the history of his success among the Bugis, the narrator emphatically disclaims all ability to recover the effect of Karain's rehearsal of his conduct toward Matara. As he says: "It is impossible to convey the effect of Karain's story. It is undying, it is but a memory, and its vividness cannot be made clear to another mind, any more than the vivid emotions of a dream" (p. 26). Such a disclaimer of narrative powers, however, at least in the immediate context of Conrad's subsequent use of the subtle Marlow as a first-person narrator, should serve only to underscore the possibility of an ironic stance. This seasoned narrator is hardly a dull-witted observer of human affairs. He may have nostalgically introduced his story with a rhapsodic reminder of "those unprotected days when we were content to hold in our hands our lives and our property" (p. 3), almost as if he would like to relive the easiness of those days, but for the most part he speaks to his listeners from the vantage point of long experience and mature reflection. Even at the time of his involvement in the gun smuggling, he has—as has been noted—perceived much of the quality behind Karain's everyday reliance upon the old sorcerer. His perception is already then sharp, and thus when he at the height of adult maturity begins his account of the final scene between Karain and the sailors with an apparent admission of the inadequacy of his own initial responses to Karain's desperate request for passage to the West, one must not immediately leap to Hollis's conclusion that the narrator's range of response as a young man is limited to ineffectual platitudes. Near the beginning of this confrontation between Karain and the sailors, the young narrator tells the native: "You must abide with your people. They need you. And there is forgetfulness in life. Even the dead cease to speak in time" (p. 43). To the reader as well as to Hollis such counsel probably appears woefully inadequate because he (like Hollis) suspects that the retreating Karain will never forget his ghost unless he achieves for himself the Conradian stature of full responsibility for his own words and deeds. And yet, to the extent that the narrator's seemingly platitudinous comment is rooted in the consciousness that Karain, despite his distress over staying among the Bugis, inextricably belongs to his own community by virtue of background and language, the narrator is eminently right. At the beginning of this confrontation between Karain and the sailors, then, the narrator's stature as a young man of insight is quite ambiguous. When Hollis takes it upon himself to provide Karain with some definite relief, however, the narrator's true mettle gradually appears.

At first, especially if one scorns the narrator's apparent ineffectuality, one may want to believe that the young Hollis can quickly resolve Karain's dilemma. One may even wish, as does Professor Johnson, to turn Hollis into a proto-Stein who "therapeutically manipulate[s] illusion" in order to save a distressed soul from the ghosts of the night.[8] More to the point, when this young seaman, by employing a Jubilee sixpence, a bit of dark blue silk ribbon, and a piece of white leather glove, concocts a new talisman for Karain, one may wish to regard his little drama as a performance inspired by "the insolent and unerring wisdom of his youth" (p. 46). Unlike the young narrator, Hollis appears to the reader to know that in a world of illusions and ghosts a good performance is essential to the success of all human effort. He appears so wise, in fact, that when he asks his fellow seamen to look serious while he enacts his brief drama, the reader may be tempted to applaud the genius of his insight and wit.

From the very beginning of the scene, however, Hollis has blurred the essential nature of the situation, the distinction between the ghostly realities that unsettle Karain in his remembrance of the past and the realities of a dramatic performance. In one breath Hollis insists, as if there is no drama but only ghosts and spirits here, that "this is no play; I am going to do something for [Karain]. Look serious"; and in the next, a bit exasperated by his friends' reluctance, he badgers them in the manner of a director: "Confound it! . . . Can't you *lie* a little . . . for a friend!" (p. 46). Obviously, even though he may initially regard his venture as morally justifiable, Hollis—much like Stein in the presence of the distressed Jim—bends to the situation and finally ignores the basic distinction between the truth and the illusion inherent in the talisman that he proffers to the distressed Karain. In that talisman Hollis himself sees both truth and illusion, but Karain sees only truth. On the surface such a difference may seem innocuous, but in essence what Hollis does here is manipulate Karain's ghosts not from Karain's but from his own perspective. In these terms, of course, especially if one faces up to its deeper moral implications, the manipulation must appear at least as questionable, if not as morally unjustifiable.

By this point it should be clear that Hollis's charm is merely another pragmatic (or stopgap) measure such as the old sorcerer's. At the end of that long final interview between Karain and the three seamen, when the sun is again rising, Karain may himself announce that Matara's ghost "has departed again—forever" (p. 51). The young narrator, too, may hope that "we [had] affirmed our faith in the power of Hollis' charm efficiently enough to put the matter beyond the shadow of a doubt." Finally, however, despite this emphasis upon success and hope, the careful reader must resist the initial appreciation of Hollis's insight and conclude that Hollis's gamelike manipulations are no more a solution to Karain's dilemma than is Stein's proffering of a ring and of Patusan a solution to Jim's. Essentially, Stein and Hollis are both preserving themselves from the poignancy of two terrible situations, not by directing Jim and Karain toward a full personal reckoning with the world of ghosts and illusions, but by offering them questionable opportunities to escape the bewildering sense of human limitation that attaches to such personal reckoning. Unlike the elder, solitary Stein, who offers his talisman in a mood of *Weltschmerz,* the young Hollis probably needs the illusion that with charms and lies he can manipulate the ghosts of the night. Whether he needs the illusion or not, however, he has somewhat foolishly manipulated Karain's affairs when it is already long past time for Karain himself, as it is for Lord Jim, to resolve the problems before him.

The young narrator's perspective, then, despite the irony that he himself later directs at its platitudes, is actually superior to that of Hollis. While the inexperienced Hollis is bent upon depriving Karain of another chance to confront a wilderness of moral emptiness (a chance that, frankly, may or may not lead Karain to a new apprehension of experience), this narrator is genuinely moved, as he later says, by the spectacle of a man who is "loyal to a vision, betrayed by his dream, spurned by his illusion, and coming to unbelievers for help—against a thought" (p. 40). He is so moved, in fact, that he finds himself speechless and unable to act. Already when the confident Hollis moves offstage in search of his box of charms, for example, the narrator discovers to his dismay, first, that he does not know "what to do with [this] problem from the outer darkness" (p. 45), and second, that he suddenly begins "to resent bitterly the hard necessity to get rid of [Karain]" (p. 46). Such disturbing feelings, however, never tempt the narrator into Hollis's stature of bold manipulator. Indeed, while Hollis prepares for his seemingly wonderful charade, this young but already shrewd narrator merely embraces the fact that illusions are the staple of life. On the surface it is a lame moment, and yet there is more to the ruminations of this narrator. In Hollis's charm he now perceives the various ghosts of the West—the shades of women, friends, ideals now forgotten or remembered—and once more reminds himself that these charms possess a *double burden* of illusion and truth, of sorrow and joy, of pain and peace (p. 40). In one passage especially, while Hollis selects appropriate trinkets from his collection, the young narrator withdraws into a philosophic mood that hints at the genius of his vision:

> Charms and talismans! Charms that keep [men] straight, that drive them crooked, that have the power to make a young man sigh, an old man smile. Potent things that procure dreams of joy, thoughts of regret; that soften hard hearts, and can temper soft ones to the hardness of steel. Gifts of heaven—things of earth. . . . (P. 48)

In such a balanced insight as this, which focuses upon the charm's potential for both good and evil, for joy and regret, the young narrator gains the courage necessary to avoid offering Karain an easy yet questionable means of salvation. In metaphysical, if not in pragmatic, terms he at least recognizes that Karain's dilemma should not be reduced to the mere manipulation of further fallible and unpredictable charms.

It is true that this profound narrator does participate in Hollis's charade and even encourages Karain to trust the younger sailor. By now it is apparent, nevertheless, that such participation is a matter not of conviction but of resignation. For while Hollis believes in the manipulation of illusions, the narrator participates in the charade only because he is aware of no alternative short of letting Karain flounder about, vulnerable to disintegration and possible suicide. Karain is not Western man, and because he will probably never understand the nature of the moral emptiness that characterizes modern, self-conscious awareness of the illusory, the narrator accepts Hollis's pragmatic, albeit somewhat insensitive, solution. The narrator may even believe (and with very good reason) that Hollis's new charm will remain efficacious. After all, because Karain does not possess modern man's appreciation of the illusory, he need never become aware of the charm's limitations—and thus face further disillusionment. Years later, however, when acknowledging his own part in the undertaking, this narrator still has not become proud of the sailors' performance. At the same time, he continues to understand its inexorable necessity. With such widely divergent attitudes, of course, it is hardly surprising that he must then resort to shrewd, muted ironies and self-ironies as the means for containing his account of Karain's history. He may appear quiet and withdrawn, even ineffectual, throughout most of that account, but by then the fact that his perspective possesses a superiority that makes of it the jewel of the story is at least clear to him. In ''Karain'' it is the narrator who serves as the vehicle of Conrad's best insight.

That this former gun-smuggling sailor has become a shrewd narrator, however, does not merely depend on the reader's appreciation of his ironies; it also appears in the tight structure of the six-chapter story. The first half of the tale centers upon Karain's activity by day (chapter 1), his activity by night (chapter 2), and finally, his arrival at the schooner amid the black thunderstorm (chapter 3); the second half, upon Karain's haphazard journey in the wilderness (chapter 4), his bewildering expectations of the narrator (chapter 5), and finally his regaining of the dawn via a new charm (chapter 6). These movements from light to black storm (chapters 1-3) and then—ironically—from the wilderness to light (chapters 4-6) clearly underscore the narrator's acute understanding of the ironies in his involvement with Karain. In the presence of such careful structure, one dares not, as does Professor Johnson, minimize the quality of his perspective, either when he is participating in Hollis's charade or when he finally narrates—some years later—the wonderful story to his friends.

Finally, then, after exposing the basis of the enormous irony in the narrator's handling of the story, I can develop the importance of this tale to Conrad's early period of sea fiction. I have already suggested that *Lord Jim* and ''The End of the Tether'' bring the early metaphor of navigation to its ironic culmination and termination. ''Karain,'' however, appears near the beginning of the period. The question, therefore, is, Why so much irony at the beginning? One likely answer is that Conrad, even as he is moving toward the brilliant use of Marlow as a navigator-narrator who enjoys successive self-realizations in Falmouth, in the Congo, and in Patusan, is very conscious that the achievement of the stature of moral navigator is a privilege not many men attain. By exploring Karain's several opportunities to confront the universe of moral emptiness, and especially by isolating—at the end of the story—the horrible ironies in Hollis's assisting of Karain, Conrad serves notice of the difficulty of achieving shrewd moral insight, no matter whether one is native or white.

At the same time, and largely as a contrast to the philosophic limitations of Karain and Hollis, Conrad provides an ironic and ambiguous narrator who becomes his most stunning achievement to date. With *The Nigger of the ''Narcissus''* and with ''Karain'' one may not be able to establish in the narrators the precise nature of the changes in perspective that later motivate their recounting of their experiences on the *Narcissus* or the gun-smuggling schooner. In responding to both tales, nevertheless, one does become conscious of the skeins of irony that ultimately define the essential narrative points of view. One does know the nature of the failures both of the crew of the *Narcissus* and of Hollis and Karain, and with such knowledge one can at least begin to appreciate the development of insight that is inherent in the narrators' discriminating ironies. With "Karain" especially, because of its surer narrative control, one is even convinced, finally, of the narrator's genuine wisdom— a wisdom that now becomes the guarantee of Conrad's continued success in his subsequent and even more convincing experiments with narrative in the three Marlow tales. In those tales Marlow fully recounts, not merely the failures of the Beards, the Kurtzes, and the Jims, but the precise nature of the growth in his own insight, which makes those failures so significant to him many years later. The new emphasis will obviously turn all three of the succeeding Marlow tales into *Bildungsromane*.

# 4

# Conrad's "Youth": Problems of Interpretation

Many readers of Conrad's "Youth" have located the climax of the conflict in personality between the old Beard and the young Marlow in the incidents immediately following the explosion of the *Judea*'s cargo in the Indian Ocean. There is, of course, a fair amount of textual evidence to support such a view. One can note, for example, that the twenty-year-old Marlow has become aware of a "queer sensation" and of an "absurd delusion" as he is "blown up" (p. 23) into the air; further, that for a time he is not even "sure whether . . . [he is] alive" after this explosion has singed off several traces of identity (his hair, eyebrows, eyelashes, and moustache); and, finally, that while the old Beard madly preoccupies himself with the wearing of tattered sails and then with the futile stripping of the worthless hulk, Marlow quickly focuses upon the possibilities for commanding—himself—a lifeboat to the closest Eastern port. These vivid details seem to suggest that, in contrast to the desperate Beard, an inexperienced but flourishing Marlow will eventually regard the final *Judea* disaster as a turning point in his career as seaman. For already now, with his perception keenly intensified and yet his identity generally uncertain, Marlow thoroughly suspends himself in the unfolding adventure as if he expects further developments and, perhaps, unusual self-realization: "This is great. I wonder what will happen" (p. 26). If, as seems likely, such expectation sharply defines the widening divergence in character between the excited mate and his exhausted captain, the expectation probably warrants the conclusion that Marlow, already in his first voyage as "a really responsible officer" (p. 5), has fully supplanted the captain as the principal officer of the ship.

To be sure, in obedience to Beard the sailors do trim the yards and they do strip the burning ship, but finally it is Marlow who provides the leadership that may save them from complete disaster. It is Marlow who initially prevents the lifeboats from smashing into the burning *Judea*; who then, after Beard has fallen asleep on a cushion with "his legs drawn up and one arm under his head" (p. 32), directs the crew from their merry repast of cheese and stout to the safety of the lifeboats; and who finally, after awakening Beard, assists the weary old man from the ship to the sailors below. The point is obvious: with the *Judea*'s sinking imminent, the young Marlow steadily meets the challenges of his office and, accepting a broad responsibility for the safety of the others, becomes the last to leave the *Judea*. In the reader's eyes at least, he has become the captain. Moreover, if such action aboard the *Judea* is not a sufficient demonstration of his new stature as captain, his performance in the cockleshell surely is: in that fourteen-foot lifeboat Marlow becomes the commander who masters the journey and brings his two men to port long before the arrival of the other lifeboats.

Such is the climax of the tale. In terms of heightened action, and especially in terms of a steady access to genuine leadership (and Beard's decline from it), there seems little question that for the young Marlow the explosion of the coal cargo has served as a turning point in his experience at sea. There is, nevertheless, a wide polarity of critical view concerning this possible seasoning of perspective.

A few critics believe that Marlow's responsible conduct immediately following the explosion, especially if taken with his other successes during the voyage, does warrant the view that he has successfully adopted for himself the rigorous code of seamanship and thus has become the commander. These critics, however, generally fail to show convincingly where or how such an adoption takes place. One of them has at least suggested that the young mate in facing a whole series of crises gradually becomes aware of the indifference of the universe and eventually matures by becoming more sober: "Marlow has outgrown the juvenile conviction of the central importance of himself to the universe; his ego has been brought within bounds."[1] Such a view, nevertheless, smacks of the insight that belongs to a wise, middle-aged Marlow—not to the restless and enthusiastic mate who races the other *Judea* seamen to the closest Eastern harbor. At age twenty, no matter how responsible he may actually have become, Marlow is not to be denied his pursuit of romance and self-importance. His ego still requires its satisfactions at the center of adventure. By suggesting that the second mate at the end of the *Judea* voyage has become a wise and sober realist before his critical and more philosophic upheaval in the Congo, this critic has yielded to the temptation of extending the growth of Marlow's perspective too far.[2]

Other critics of "Youth" have entirely avoided the view that Marlow "grows." Walter F. Wright, for example, has suggested that in the tale "there is no revolution of character"[3] at all. He construes the young Marlow's enthusiastic behavior at the end of the story as the conduct of an officer who still has much to learn both about his profession and about life itself, and thus he entirely discounts the possibility that the mate has achieved a new level of professional insight. It is Murray Krieger, however, who seems to make the strongest case against the young Marlow. At first Krieger finds himself reluctant to put any interpretation at all on the young Marlow's conduct. Because the elder Marlow always appears to disparage any suggestion of respectability in the *Judea*'s affairs, Krieger argues, "there is difficulty in our taking . . . [the young Marlow] seriously throughout the tale any more than we take seriously his 'first command,' his captaincy of the lifeboat at the end."[4] And yet, while Krieger tries to chart a neutral course by regarding the story as an unresolved tension between the young Marlow's romanticism and the elder Marlow's realism,[5] the effect of all his concentration upon the elder Marlow's playful skepticism is that his discussion, too, diminishes the possibility for growth in the young Marlow.

Perhaps the best way out of this sharp conflict between two critical extremes is to assume that the "truth" about the young Marlow lies somewhere in between. Such an assumption possesses the advantages both of leading toward a reconciliation of the views, each of which has some textual weight behind it, and of encouraging a fresh perception of the story. In order to facilitate this reconciliation, however, it is first necessary to reexamine in detail the nature of Conrad's narrative technique within the story. Krieger's conclusion that the elder Marlow's skepticism can only demean the respectability of the *Judea*'s voyage (and thus of the young Marlow's experience) is very serious. Only by answering that objection can I proceed to a discussion of a specific change of attitude that may warrant the view that the young Marlow has matured. In this chapter, then, I intend to focus upon two problems of interpretation: (1) the problem of narrative technique, and (2) the problem of defining the precise nature of the young Marlow's maturation upon the *Judea*. Such focusing will offer a new, more comprehensive perspective from which to view the young Marlow's *Judea* experience.

The technique that Conrad employs in developing "Youth" has confounded his readers as much as it has intrigued them. There is in the tale a first-person narrator who recounts how Marlow reminisces about his first journey as second mate. Such a pattern of narrative relationships turns out to be very impressionistic because it offers Conrad an opportunity to present his material through two raconteurs, the second of whom—Marlow—is somewhat less disciplined than the first. The gain in such presentation centers upon the elder Marlow: while the unidentified but more conventional narrator probably recalls as exactly as possible the episodes that Marlow reminisces about, Marlow himself indulges in a loose, even whimsical recounting of the various crises[6] that he has endured during his year's duty on the *Judea*. Such indulging obviously makes the elder Marlow a principal in the tale as a whole, for it allows Marlow to direct as much irony at his present self as he directs at his younger self. For example, instead of acknowledging that his present attitude toward his *Judea* experience is one of respect and appreciation, this elder Marlow may decide to adopt a disparaging attitude toward that experience in order to avoid a tone that even among close friends may seem too self-serving. At the same time he (and surely Conrad) may realize that such an attitude also increases his friends' involvement in the recital. In fact, unless his friends pick up this fundamentally ironic, self-deprecatory stance and interpret all of Marlow's comments about his involvement in the various *Judea* episodes in relation to it, they will arrive at much the same conclusion that Krieger has reached. The friends, nevertheless, even if they have not previously heard the precise details, probably suspect (and maybe even know) how much the voyage as second mate has transformed the younger Marlow's attitudes. In their presence the elder Marlow can confidently play his subtle narrative game.

The use of the narrator-within-a-narrator is, then, more complicated than Krieger implies. With a Marlow who is capable of irony directed at both past and present selves narrating the tale, there is a good chance that all the scoffing at his earlier experience upon the *Judea* is designed to heighten the dramatic effects of the story and thus—at least from Conrad's point of view—to involve his readers fully in the story. That Marlow is playing a subtle narrative game is probably most evident in his use of such devices as sentimentality and hyperbole throughout the story. Both devices now bear brief consideration.

The elder Marlow, while indulging himself in the bottle, several times easily relaxes into a rather sentimental appreciation of the vitality of youth. On the surface the implication of such appreciation seems to be that youth, not maturation, is at the heart of his present reminiscing. In at least one moment the paean to youth that Marlow delivers is particularly rhapsodic on this point:

> Oh, the glamour of youth! Oh, the fire of it, more dazzling than the flames of the burning [*Judea*], throwing a magic light on the wide earth, leaping audaciously to the sky, presently to be quenched by time, more cruel, more pitiless, more bitter than the sea—and like the flames of the burning ship surrounded by an impenetrable night. (P. 30)

The essential feeling within this rhapsody may be that youth is precious, perhaps more precious than any maturation to a life of responsibility and its deadening of enthusiasm and interest. At the same time, however, there seems to be another, more subtle feeling implicit within the inflation of the passage—the feeling that the intensities of youth may be recovered in the sentimental emotionalism of middle age. By lamenting in grandiloquent fashion the loss of his youth (toward the end of the tale this Marlow will become even more eloquent upon the unalterable fact of such loss), the elder Marlow may be contriving to regain at least a spurious sense of his emotional intensity as a twenty-year-old second mate. Obviously, the wise Marlow is aware of the impossibility of such recovery, and yet, probably in order to give a sense of his strong feeling for the *Judea* voyage without appearing too self-serving, he adopts the device of an easy sentimentalism that knows no bounds—a device that certainly heightens the dramatic effect but that also introduces an essential irony at nearly every juncture of the story.

Another major device that is operating in the passage quoted above, and that Marlow uses extensively for ironic or humorous effects, is hyperbole. Here it is possible to isolate, by way of example, Marlow's handling of the gale episode three hundred miles west of the Lizards.

There an Atlantic gale batters the ship unmercifully for more than a week, and when the *Judea* begins to leak, all the sailors—Marlow included—become involved in the back-breaking labors of pumping around the clock. The gale's threat is staggering, and by listening to the elder Marlow one gets a full sense of its oppressiveness: "The world was nothing but an immensity of great foaming waves rushing at us, under a sky low enough to touch with the hand and dirty like a smoked ceiling" (p. 10). The sky is dark and very low, but here the figurative language—especially the smoked ceiling—belongs primarily to the elder Marlow's determination to recover the emotional quality of the situation now years in the past. The *Judea*'s situation has unquestionably troubled the inexperienced second mate too, for during the crisis he is quite surprised to discover himself as "lasting it out as well as any of these men and keeping [his] chaps up to the mark" (p. 12). For the elder Marlow, however, this crisis has over the years become something much more than the mere occasion for self-realization. For him it has become a metaphysical "immensity." To be sure, he will always regard the crisis as one of those important moments that in retrospect and from the vantage point of a distinguished career define the watersheds of his moral experience. And yet, precisely because this Atlantic gale has encouraged his growth into a genuine seaman, he cannot now avoid the delicious temptation of embellishing the episode and making the gale one of the most horrendous storms of all time:

> There was for us no sky, there were for us no stars, no sun, no universe—nothing but angry clouds and an infuriated sea.... [the gale] seemed to last for months, for years, for all eternity, as though we had been dead and gone to a hell for sailors. We forgot the day of the week, the name of the month, what year it was, and whether we had ever been ashore. (Pp. 11—12)

By virtue of such embellishment the elder Marlow somewhat whimsically pits his younger self against metaphysical dimensions (nothingness and timelessness) of which that self has very little appreciation—at least not at age twenty, when he is still ten years away from his journey into the Congo. These dimensions, therefore, should strike the reader as rather humorous and even ridiculous—or as further means whereby Marlow can approach the truth of his past experience without appearing too self-serving.

By now it is clear that the elder Marlow's ironies and embellishments, all of which are designed to avoid a self-serving tone, should not deflect the reader from an appreciation of Marlow's actual growth during the *Judea* voyage. The fact that Marlow does not objectively recount both the serious dangers that threaten the *Judea* on her final trip and the difference that this voyage has made in his own successful career is not evidence, as Krieger implies, that Marlow is demeaning his conduct as second mate. On the contrary, with his engaging assumption of tones that are grandiose and strikingly sentimental, humorous and ironic, Marlow indicates, to his friends at least, how much he still appreciates the importance of the *Judea* voyage to his career. It is true that the elder Marlow may also enjoy the mere opportunity of regaling others with his subtleties and thus that he probably "edits" his experiences on the spur of the moment for any heightened effect he may suddenly conceive of. Nevertheless, the convincing manner with which he freely handles his material consistently reflects both a sureness of his own understanding of his *Judea* experience and an inner confidence that his listeners (especially the four seamen sitting around the mahogany table with him) will immediately reach, without his having to make an explicit statement, the same understanding. Conrad expects of his readers no less an understanding.

There is in addition to the confusion surrounding the elder Marlow's narrative irony a great deal of critical uncertainty about the precise nature of the young Marlow's maturation. Many readers, for example, aware of the second mate's seemingly unwavering enthusiasm for romance, have reacted very skeptically to the proposition that the second mate experiences genuine maturation during this voyage of the *Judea*. In fact, even though these readers may now appreciate the nature of the elder Marlow's double self-irony, they probably will not forget that the young mate at the beginning of the voyage is excited about being a "really responsible officer" for the first time and that he perceives a "touch of romance" in the old ruined ship, in her motto of Do or Die, and in her destination to the "magic" and "blessed" Bangkok. Nor will they forget that Marlow later in the voyage suspends himself above immediate concern for his own safety in the romantic excitement of full participation in a succession of disasters. Consider the Lizards' disaster, for instance. Marlow regards that episode as the "deuce of an adventure," as the drama in which he can transform the tossing *Judea* from a "rattle-trap" into "the test, the trial of life" itself. Or he regards the explosion in the Indian Ocean as another "great" adventure in which the furious burning of the *Judea* becomes a "magnificent" and "glorious" death. Such romantic regard seems to leave the mate completely open to the accusation of romantic escapism. In all these instances, however, the elder Marlow may again merely be seeking striking narrative effects through sentimentalism or hyperbole. Clearly, one cannot argue that the young Marlow entirely ignores the immediate and very real dangers before him. After all, in the Lizards' disaster and then in the Indian Ocean he does perform his duties well and at those points even becomes conscious of having achieved some wonderful self-realization.

In a frequently overlooked section of the story — the six-month delay at Falmouth for extensive repairs following the Lizards' gale — Conrad provides a key episode for better understanding the complex relationship between the young mate's ardent romanticism and his professional development. Until Falmouth Marlow has romantically expected all his action to be adventurous and significant, as befits both his appointment to official duty and his long-awaited journeying to the East, but with the interminable harboring of the *Judea* he can perceive in his largely unnecessary and seemingly meaningless overseeing of the rigging nothing of romance or self-realization. To his chagrin, furthermore, he must witness how after a time the people of Falmouth, even the small boys playing in the water, reduce his beloved ship to an object of scorn and of humiliating ridicule. He himself feels the derision, and at that point the long weeks of repairs and delays become an awkward period of some desperation that he may interrupt by taking a short, five-day holiday to London but that he can never entirely escape short of throwing up his berth. In Falmouth, consequently, the heretofore exuberant Marlow increasingly tires of his official position, and ultimately he feels himself entirely outside the center of romance and importance: "It seemed as though we [Marlow and Beard and Mahon] had been forgotten by the world, belonged to nobody, would get nowhere" (p. 16). The negative quality of this feeling defines the low point in Marlow's *Judea* experience.

Some months thereafter, however, when the *Judea* finally renews her slow way to the East, the young and weary Marlow reveals a rather important change in attitude. For then, instead of continuing to invest the old ship with the heavy romance that he had perceived in her before the long dry-docking in Falmouth, he becomes as conscious of her weariness as he is of his own tedium during the past six months. Indeed, in the face of his new insight into the *Judea*'s grave physical limitations (she travels "at the rate of three miles an hour"), he himself now begins to feel a bit out of sorts with his long-admired ship: "it seemed as though we had been born in [the *Judea*], reared in her, had lived in her for ages" (p. 18). This passage, of course, recovers much of Marlow's feeling in Falmouth, and thus it is clear that whether he is dry-docked and forgotten or again sailing slowly through the Atlantic, Marlow consistently perceives time as "an interminable procession of days" or, in other words, as a dead-level, glamourless continuum of insignificant events. To be sure, with the *Judea*'s sudden diminishing of stature to a rattletrap, he may not have lost all his earlier penchant for romantic enthusiasm, but it is now certain that if he is to avoid becoming a casualty of indifference or of madness,[7] he here faces the necessity of a further adjustment in attitude toward the old ship and toward time. That adjustment, by enabling him to balance the realities of everyday time with his romantic fervor, will constitute the precise change of attitude that underlies his maturation aboard the *Judea*.

Marlow makes his important adjustment when, in a final effort to appreciate his old and weary ship, he enlarges his conception of the significance of the journey: "I thought of men of old who, centuries ago, went that road in ships that sailed no better" (p. 18). At first glance this recollection may seem another flight into romantic fantasy, particularly if one concentrates upon Marlow's allusions to the "palms" and "spices" and "yellow sands" of the ancient navigators, and yet the principal sense of the passage is that the second mate has experienced a moment of professional self-realization that is of considerably more significance than his self-realization near the Lizards. For after surviving the awkward period at Falmouth in which only a lingering respect for his new office has bolstered his courage aboard an object of scorn, he now discovers that there is a long and continuous tradition of sea voyagers who have, each in his turn, endured their own periods of distress "in ships that sailed no better."[8] For him, therefore, the seaman's legacy suddenly includes both the romance and the tedium of the journey, and it is on this new basis that he accepts—contentedly—the present necessity of the *Judea*'s slow progress toward the East.

The elder Marlow in a moment of characteristic self-depreciation may disparage the second mate's contented resumption of the journey as living "the life of youth in ignorance and hope," and yet the seasoning effect of this realization concerning the seaman's legacy must not be overlooked. Such seasoning is already apparent in the passage immediately preceding the young Marlow's recollection of the old navigators' experience. For then, after having for months silently bemoaned his ill fate in being forgotten on the hapless *Judea*, the second mate becomes reconciled to her inadequacies and to the leisurely satisfaction of his desire for adventure: "There was all the East before me, and all life, and the thought that I had been tried in that ship and had come out pretty well" (p. 18). Once more the young mate is conscious of self-realization, this time not merely in his having successfully endured a gale near the Lizards, but in his having achieved a larger temporal perspective from which to appreciate his service upon the *Judea*. With such consciousness, his anxiety over the tedium of duty aboard a rattletrap ship gradually dissipates. More importantly, however, he now possesses something of a guarantee: if he can fulfill the professional, yet often boring, duties of his office, he can still anticipate — and then freely embrace — those periodic moments of adventure for which his young spirit longs. It is not much of a guarantee, but already in the Indian Ocean he knows its efficacy.

The six months' delay in Falmouth, then, because it provides the young Marlow with a bitter interruption of his glorious journey to the East and with a ripening of professional attitude,[9] becomes the crucial period in the growth of the mate's perspective aboard the *Judea*. To be sure, this Marlow has not yet fully comprehended the indifference of the universe (as does the Marlow of *Heart of Darkness*), nor has he approached the urbane steadiness of middle age (as does the Marlow of *Lord Jim*), but he has assumed the seaman's legacy of the importance even of everyday routine. Such an assumption, therefore, not only prepares him for ready acceptance of life with or without robust adventure, but it also enables the reader to appreciate (in the climax of the story) the magnitude of Marlow's achievement as he with his attention to duty saves the *Judea*'s officers and crew from the potential disasters following the explosion of her cargo. Far from performing wonderfully only because of the adventure in the crisis, as the demeaning irony of the elder Marlow might suggest, the young Marlow reveals himself then as the consummate master who both executes the essentials of responsibility and savors his exciting opportunity for further adventure and self-realization. Indeed, while Beard sleeps and the others eat and drink, it is Marlow who becomes the ship's most eloquent representative of the seaman's tradition.

That Marlow is one of the fortunate who achieve the heights of the seaman's tradition is also apparent — again despite the elder Marlow's ironic exposure of his racing antics — in the cockleshell's journey toward the Javanese harbor. During that hard trip the second mate once more has reason to exult both in the accomplishment of his duty and in the access to further self-confidence based on his new achievement: "I did not know how good a man I was till then" (p. 36). It is true, of course, that in his first contact with the East (with the skipper of the *Celestial*) Marlow endures the humiliation of being called "Pig" and thus of almost being convinced that he had "sinned against the harmony of the universe" (p. 39), and further, that he becomes aware that the light at the end of the jetty (about which the *Celestial*'s skipper is so angry) is out and thus that the world is still potentially "black." For Marlow, nevertheless, the East is not a world of curses and darkness. Even if he is exhausted, he is probably already quite aware that the *Judea* voyage promises much for his future. Indeed, once he is in the harbor, he rather quickly comes to professional terms with his new surroundings: "This was the East of the ancient navigators, so old, so mysterious, resplendent and sombre, living and unchanged, full of danger and promise" (p. 41). Having successfully completed his cockleshell voyage to Java Head, Marlow may now even regard himself—at least potentially—as one of the great navigators who inhabit the glorious world "full of danger and promise." Self-satisfied, exhilarated with high romance, he breathes deeply the pleasant and aromatic breezes from the Eastern woods. The fragrance is his reward.

The next morning, furthermore, while the other *Judea* personnel, wearied by their journey, sleep in "careless attitudes of death," the young and confident Marlow awakens in a flood of brilliant light to a sky that "had never looked so far, so high, before." In this huge and sensuous world of possibility his color-starved eyes immediately begin to soak up all the dazzling beauty of the wide harbor: "the glittering sands, the wealth of green infinite and varied, the sea blue like the sea of a dream, the crowd of attentive faces, the blaze of vivid colour — the water reflecting it all" (p. 41). In such a passage one cannot escape the fact that this young but matured commander has awakened to the new day in his life and its promise of even further adventure and self-realization. In "Youth," therefore, already before *Heart of Darkness* and *Lord Jim*, the young Marlow has become — despite whatever self-deprecatory constructions the sentimental and ironic elder Marlow may place upon his behavior throughout the tale — a genuine representative of the navigator's tradition.

# 5

## Navigation in *Heart of Darkness*

Near the end of the first two sections of Conrad's *Heart of Darkness* the Marlow who has slowly been penetrating into the heart of the Congo experiences nothing less than a revelation about the significance of articulating within the wilderness surrounding him. Toward the end of the first section, for example, while engaging in the long interview with the brickmaker (who pumps Marlow for privileged information concerning Kurtz), Marlow becomes conscious of himself as an imposter, specifically a "prevaricator," by virtue of his quiet solicitude for a Kurtz whom he does not even know. In fact, because the plotting brickmaker does not perceive the nature of Marlow's allegiance, the interview becomes the occasion not only for Marlow's deception of the brickmaker, but also for his bewildering realization of the probable futility underlying any articulation or formulation of experience in such a wilderness context. As the elder Marlow narrates:

> The smell of mud, of primeval mud, by Jove! was in my nostrils, the high stillness of primeval forest was before my eyes. . . . All this was great, expectant, mute, while the [brickmaker] jabbered about himself. I wondered whether the stillness on the face of the immensity looking at us two were meant as an appeal or a menace. What were we who had strayed in here? Could we handle that dumb thing, or would it handle us? I felt how big, how confoundedly big, was that thing that couldn't talk and perhaps was deaf as well. What was in there? (P. 27)

Already conscious for some time of his status as an imposter, at least ever since he accepted his role as steamer captain for an enterprise bringing "civilization" to a dark Congo, this relatively young—probably thirtyish if one can rely, here, upon biographical data from Conrad's own life—captain now discovers a much larger spatial and temporal universe than he has ever known. This universe, clearly enough, is the typical Conradian wilderness or sea in which there is never an objective sanction for a character's word or deed and in which, consequently, a character such as Marlow at best becomes conscious of himself only as manipulating a precarious and uncertain tissue of relationship to an incomprehensible world. Indeed, as the jabbering manipulator of an indefinable and seemingly unnavigable immensity, he also becomes conscious of his life as the ultimate futility or absurdity.

This realization, however, serves only as the basis for a second critical discovery. Near the end of the second section of the novel, after having in fact navigated his dilapidated steamer through the fog and the natives' attack, Marlow anticipates the probability of Kurtz's death and at that point senses in himself an "extreme disappointment, as though [he] had found out [that he] had been striving after something altogether without a substance" (pp. 47-48). Marlow, it must be remembered, allied himself with Kurtz following his encounter with the meddlesome brickmaker, and throughout his journey from the Central to the Inner Station he has, in addition to "feeling" the wilderness, been conscious of approaching "exclusively" a Kurtz whose eloquence promises a significant moral alternative to the bickering and backbiting of the jabbering pilgrims. Kurtz's probable death, therefore, exposes him to a sudden and "startling extravagance of emotion." As he later relates to his listeners, "I couldn't have felt more of lonely desolation somehow, had I been robbed of a belief or had missed my destiny in life" (p. 48). Marlow has expected from the eloquent Kurtz some definition of the sanctions according to which man may organize his experience in the jabbering wilderness of a modern world, and thus his sense of loss probably refers not so much to his failure in reaching Kurtz as to his present entrapment in a universe without moral definition.

In fact, without denying the possible edge of Marlow's grief for Kurtz the man, one must realize here that the Marlow who has already confronted the deaf and dumb wilderness now faces the further necessity of superseding all formulations of reality that Kurtz may, or may not, have provided: without Kurtz as the potential oracle of human experience the captain now, for the first time, understands that he must chart his own course through the Congo wilderness. It is this understanding that lies at the heart of the narrating Marlow's most important comment in the novel:

> The earth for [most of] us is a place to live in, where we must put up with sights, with sounds, with smells, too, by Jove!—breathe dead hippo, so to speak, and not be contaminated. And there, don't you see? Your strength comes in, the faith in your ability for the digging of unostentatious holes to bury the stuff in—your power of devotion, not to yourself, but to an obscure, back-breaking business. (P. 50)

For men who are neither foolish nor exalted—that is, for most men according to Marlow—this passage graphically details the process of articulation, whether physical or verbal or even preverbal, which is necessary for "creating" an existence in a moral wilderness. Another implication in the passage, however, is this: if only by virtue of its position in the novel, the passage suggests that the Marlow who now reaches the Inner Station finally understands what strength and devotion (to "lying") the process of articulation entails, and thus that—even before he discovers that Kurtz is yet alive—his maturation of philosophic insight is essentially complete.

Generally, however, critics of *Heart of Darkness* have ignored the significance of the conclusion to the novel's middle section and have, instead, made much of the interview between Marlow and Kurtz in the third. About a decade ago, for example, Kenneth Bruffee argued that Marlow's perception of Kurtz's final utterance is both a "reward" and a "penalty," for in that moment the captain achieves the stature of shrewd moral insight by acknowledging the fundamental horror in human experience—the horror that man must inhabit a wilderness without absolute sanctions.[1] Many readers of the novel have since agreed with Bruffee, and recently, taking a new and more emphatic direction, a couple of critics have provided even further support for such a position. One of them, James Guetti, in a brilliant discussion of the philosophic limits of Conrad's language and metaphor, has pointed out that as a key to the novel one must approach Kurtz's struggle and utterance in terms not of moral "truth" but of the difficulty of finding a verbal equivalent or correlative in an "alinguistic" wilderness.[2] Even if one accepts Guetti's basic suggestion (and certainly the suggestion provides much of the

foundation for my commentary on Marlow's early recognition of himself as a liar), however, one still must consider whether Guetti is right in
further assuming that Marlow's most crucial moments of self-realization
occur *after* he reaches the Inner Station. Similarly, one must question
Bruce Johnson's assertion, itself based upon Guetti's argument, that
Marlow's decision to lie to the Intended is "a tribute to *the new sense of
responsibility Kurtz's victory has taught him, a sense that does not en-
courage us to pursue magic names that are somehow already intrinsic
but to give names in a new spirit.*"[3] By detailing Marlow's reactions to
names during his Congo venture, Johnson shrewdly exposes the subjective character of the sanctions by which Marlow organizes his moral experience in the last section of the novel. Much in the manner of Bruffee
and Guetti, nevertheless, he ignores the possibility that Marlow's
maturation is essentially complete with his radical perceptions at the end
of sections one and two, that is, before he witnesses Kurtz's final
victory.

That Marlow experiences such a full development before he reaches
the Inner Station, then, requires further elaboration. In order to demonstrate such development, I intend, first, to explore the theme and the
metaphor of navigation in the novel and, second, to show how this
metaphor creates for us a thorough and heretofore unrecognized ironic
reading of Marlow's involvement with Kurtz and the Intended.


I have already established the fact that Conrad had definite and sometimes very bitter opinions about the industrial progress that during his
lifetime transformed the craftsmanship of journeying out to sea. I have
also noted how these opinions color the artistic rendering of many of his
past experiences—especially those difficult periods of service upon
steamers. Here one need only recall Conrad's reactions to serving upon
the *Vidar* late in 1887, an experience that becomes the basis for Captain
Whalley's disconcerting *Sofala* trip in "The End of the Tether," or his
reactions to serving upon the *Roi des Belges* in 1890, the experience
that becomes the basis for Marlow's difficulties in *Heart of Darkness*.
In both cases Conrad himself knew the demoralization of having accepted the strictures of service for which he had little respect. As might
be expected, therefore, even in the fictional account of those experiences the office of steamer captain represents—for both the principal
characters (Whalley and Marlow)—"the last resort," the last viable

choice following the sale of the *Fair Maid* or the unsuccessful six-month search for another sailing berth to the Far East. Once such an office is accepted, furthermore, both captains (much like Conrad himself) almost necessarily become conscious of themselves as the unfortunate, even if willing, captives of a mechanical monotony and an attendant personal deterioration that lies well beyond their previous experience.

For Conrad, however, this monotony and deterioration possess even larger metaphysical implications—implications that quickly become apparent if I again, briefly, isolate the theme of ship mechanization in *The Mirror of the Sea*. Early in that volume, while commenting upon the stolidity of a steamer, Conrad reveals a strong disdain that goes to the heart of his views on modern seamanship: "[The steamer] makes her passages on other principles than yielding to the weather and humouring the sea. She receives smashing blows, but she advances; it is a slogging fight, and not a scientific campaign. The machinery, the steel, the fire, the steam have stepped in between the man and the sea" (*MS*, p. 72). The reader's appreciation of the disdain in the passage depends upon his grasping the significance, for Conrad, of this separation between man and the sea. In an earlier passage in *The Mirror* Conrad elaborates upon the results of such separation and concludes that service upon a steamship is not an art:

> It is less personal and a more exact calling; less arduous, but also less gratifying in the lack of close communication between the artist and the medium of his art. It is, in short, less a matter of love. . . . It is an occupation which a man not desperately subject to seasickness can be imagined to follow with content, without enthusiasm, with industry, without affection. (*MS*, P. 30)

The implicit contrast in this passage between the nature of service upon a sailing ship and that upon a steamer obviously underscores one of the fundamental assumptions, that sailing is a fine art, behind Conrad's use of navigational metaphor throughout his fiction from *The Nigger of the "Narcissus"* to "The End of the Tether." In addition, such a contrast may point to the possibility that for both Whalley and Marlow the shift from sails to steam will develop into a terrible crisis of vocation and, perhaps, of vision too. In these terms, of course, the shift from sails to steam becomes a profound key even to understanding a work set in the wilderness yet belonging to this period—*Heart of Darkness*.

At the beginning of *Heart of Darkness*, when Marlow exchanges his profession as a saltwater sailor for a stint of freshwater steaming up the

Congo River, the reader must recognize that Conrad is essentially isolating Marlow's experience as a paradigm for what is happening to man in the transition from a traditional to a modern world. To be sure, the reader has no firm knowledge of Marlow's past experience, other than that it has occurred upon the open sea, but if he recognizes that Marlow's sudden switch to freshwater steaming is rooted in Conrad's own experience, he can probably assume with some assurance—but leaving the text as the final arbiter—that this Marlow who has just returned from six years of navigating the seas of the Far East is fundamentally a saltwater sailor. As such a sailor, Marlow is in Conrad's world making a switch of profound consequence when he accepts service in the Congo. Conrad, of course, may not be implying by his isolation of Marlow's vocational switch Marlow's moral degeneration into, say, the amorphous lassitude of the "pilgrims," but he is suggesting that this switch presents Marlow with a critical choice: either allegiance to traditional values of seamanship or absorption into the moral confusion of his peers in the company. In other words, Marlow faces the transition from a world of sailing, where the sanctions of tradition provide moral direction during long voyages, to the world of steaming, where mechanization has by shortening and regularizing the routes of navigation nullified much of the significance of such sanctions. In the Congo wilderness saltwater traditions possess no objective validity. There, consequently, the pressure is upon Marlow, as the representative of man in a world of transition, to discover what limited subjective validity they may yet possess—hence Conrad's emphasis throughout the tale upon Marlow's "navigation" of a wilderness world.

That *navigation* is an appropriate term for defining Marlow's penetration into the Congo becomes even clearer if one remembers the frame of the tale. At the very beginning, before Marlow begins his narration, and while the five friends are waiting for the turn of the tide in the Thames, the first-person narrator emphasizes the darkness of London (a theme that Marlow shortly thereafter broadens into a dominant equation between England and the Congo) and then focuses upon the great tradition of the Thames, the tradition of Sir Francis Drake and Sir John Franklin, "the great knights-errant of the sea" (p. 4). Both of these adventurous explorers, according to this narrator, are "bearers of a spark from the sacred fire," and as such bearers they may function as precursors of the pilgrims (and thus of Kurtz and Marlow) who bear the "torch of civilization" into the Congo. In the face of Conrad's own consistent appreciation of such navigators and explorers,[4] however, the reader must recognize already at the beginning that the sacred fire of Drake and Franklin can hardly be that of the pilgrims. For the true navigators, instead of trying to subdue a world into subjection or conformity, are bent only upon exploring and advancing the boundaries of human knowledge. Marlow, too, is appreciative of this sense of the tradition:

> Now when I was a little chap I had a passion for maps. I would look for hours at South America, or Africa, or Australia, and lose myself in all the glories of exploration. At that time there were many blank spaces on the earth, and when I saw one that looked particularly inviting on a map (but they all look that) I would put my finger on it and say, When I grow up I will go there. (P. 8)[5]

By the time Marlow reaches manhood, however, navigators have explored and defined many of these blank spaces of his childhood. As he himself points out, even the Congo "had got filled since my boyhood with rivers and lakes and names. It had ceased to be a blank space of delightful mystery — a white patch for a boy to dream gloriously over. . . . [But] there was in it one river especially, a mighty big river, . . . And as I looked at the map of it in a shop window, [the river] fascinated me as a snake would a bird — a silly little bird" (p. 8). Even in his maturity, it is clear, the Marlow who already has seen a good many places of the earth retains much of his childhood emotion concerning exploration. The result of such retention, at least with his assignment to the captaincy of a steamer on the Congo River, is that he himself finally becomes a participant in the rich tradition of navigation and exploration that has engrossed him for so many years.

To be sure, Marlow does not advance man's knowledge of the physical details of the Congo. His serious bout with fever terminates that glamorous possibility.[6] What Marlow does become conscious of in the Congo is his journey into "the night of the first ages" — into the darkness of the self, which, according to Wylie Sypher, "must be intuited in the dim and quiet eddies streaming like quicksands far below the mechanism of the rational mind, which is forever falsifying our experience by its clear and intelligible logic.'"[7] Such a journey for Conrad the writer, nevertheless, is an exploration of as much validity, if not objectivity, as is inherent in the journeys of Drake and Franklin. Consequently, when Marlow points out that this Congo journey "was the farthest point of navigation and the culminating point of [his] experience" (p. 7), his Congo experience must be recognized as belonging, despite its subjectivity, to the rich tradition of navigators before him.

Upon entering the Congo as Conrad's navigator of the wilderness of self, Marlow immediately and for many months thereafter encounters radically new stimuli and situations that threaten and undermine his allegiance to saltwater traditions. At one point, however, having already observed some of the metaphysical implications within the prehistoric universe beyond the Central Station, he rather conservatively reacts to the discovery of the Russian harlequin's *An Inquiry into some Points of Seamanship:* "I handled this amazing antiquity with the greatest possible tenderness, lest it should dissolve in my hands. . . . [The book] made me forget the jungle and the pilgrims in a delicious sensation of having come upon *something unmistakably real*" (pp. 38–39; emphasis added). Here, by virtue of his relief at having found a reminder of his past life as a sailor in the Far East, Marlow, despite his present bewilderment, betrays a continued allegiance to the heroic traditions of navigation in sails. Momentarily escaping the confusion of the explorations immediately before him, in fact, he finds that the handling of the book essentially reaffirms the qualities of seamanship (such as steadfastness and reliability) that no longer obtain in the wilderness of the modern world. By providing such a reaffirmation, of course, such a discovery probably prepares for Marlow's eventual success in bringing the steamer through to the Inner Station. For just as he now admires the author's "singleness of intention, an honest concern for the right way of going to work" (p. 38), so Marlow himself will in the next two days of horrifying distress manage to persevere in the best manner of the ageless tradition of seamanship. Some years later the narrating Marlow will point out toward the end of section one: "I don't like work — no man does — but I like what is in work, — the chance to find yourself. Your own reality — for myself, not for others — what no other man can ever know" (p. 29). Such a passage reflects the wisdom of experience. In the Congo this captain has wandered into the wilderness of self, but with a steadfastness of purpose and intention that is the hallmark of the great navigator he has journeyed out of the very depths of that reality a better man.

There are three episodes of navigation in the novel that reveal the essential quality of Marlow's explorations and self-realizations in the Congo. The first episode appears in the first section of the story when Marlow sets out on a fifteen-day journey with a caravan of sixty men toward the Central Station, where he expects to assume his command.

The narrative context of that episode is rather short, and thus it is probably crucial in that context that one also remember all the uneasiness and the self-doubt that from the beginning of the tale have deflected Marlow from full concentration upon his new vocational undertaking. For if one recognizes that Marlow's repeated perception of himself as an imposter at the company's headquarters in Brussels foreshadows his entrapment within a wilderness devoid of moral sanction, one can readily understand the significance of what happens in his first attempt at navigation.

While leading the caravan toward the Central Station, Marlow is, above all, conscious of the confusion before him. During the day there are paths leading everywhere, and during the night he hears "the tremor of far-off drums, sinking, swelling, a tremor vast, faint; a sound weird, appealing, suggestive, and wild—and perhaps with as profound a meaning as the sound of bells in a Christian country" (p. 20). The confusion of the paths and of the drums, however, is only a preliminary for Marlow's developing awareness of the inadequacy of vocational sanctions. For now he encounters a drunken white man who interrupts the caravan's progress and declares that he is looking after the upkeep of the road. Like Marlow with his riverboat assignment, this white man seems to possess an objective, vocational sanction for his conduct, but as Marlow pursues his journey toward the Central Station, he discovers the fraudulent nature of the man's vocation: "Can't say I saw any road or any upkeep, unless the body of a middle-aged negro, with a bullet-hole in the forehead, upon which I absolutely stumbled three miles farther on, may be considered as a permanent improvement" (p. 20). Then, sometime later, he becomes conscious of the fact that the native bearers of the other white man, who is faint and fat, begin to run away from their questionably sanctioned vocational duties (they have been "forced" to duty). At that point, confronting the possibility of "quite a mutiny," a possibility that he can arrest only by making "a speech in English with gestures" (p. 21) that the natives do not understand, he for the first time perceives the fundamental futility of his own assertion of vocation in a wilderness of confusion. The next morning, in fact, when he realizes that the bearers have wrecked the "whole concern" in the undergrowth despite his speech, and thus that the saltwater traditions by which he has tried to organize the natives' and even his own Congo life no longer possess any efficacy, Marlow (perhaps in the manner of the drunken roadkeeper and the faint comrade) feels himself becoming

"scientifically interesting," that is, fully threatened and disillusioned. That feeling, especially if coupled with his discovery a short time later that his steamer lies at the bottom of the river, surely entails the loss of his own stature as captain and thus of all the vocational sanctions by which man tries to organize his experience. The upshot is that Marlow now becomes fully vulnerable to the possibility of a thorough moral upheaval.

To be sure, Marlow does not find himself completely divorced from the tradition of seamanship. By disciplining himself, he yet manages to invest the virtually meaningless vocational sanctions with a very personal subjective validity that already reflects in him some growth of perspective. In the face of the loss of his steamer, for example, Marlow deliberately waits for the rivets and ultimately manages to repair the steamer and to prepare her for further navigational ventures in the Congo. Despite such success, nevertheless, Marlow at the Central Station continues to become more isolated, if only spatially, from the more objective supports inherent in the tradition that has, as one learns in "Youth," developed over the course of several thousand years and that, even though dying, still prevails in the service of sails. In the middle section of the story, therefore, when Marlow engages in the two-month navigation from the Central to the Inner Station, one must anticipate the probability that his separation from tradition and its vocational sanctions — a separation again graphically represented in the metaphor — will achieve an even greater intensity. Consider, for instance, the fact that during the journey to the Inner Station Marlow will operate not so much by the skill of seamanship as by the luck of inspiration: "I had to keep guessing at the channel; I had to discern, mostly by inspiration, the signs of hidden banks; I watched for sunken stone" (p. 34). On that journey Marlow witnesses the increasing breakdown of the timeworn operational procedures that characterize the craft of the sea, and with that breakdown he becomes further trapped in a dark, confusing, bewildering world whose outlines defy accurate perception or absolute understanding. As a consequence, he faces the necessity of making some radical adjustments of perspective.

With the thorough breakdown of the tradition of seamanship at least in an objective sense, of course, it is quite natural that Marlow should regard his voyage to the Inner Station as tantamount to "travelling back to the earliest beginnings of the world" (p. 34) — to the origins of all traditions and standards of conduct. During this voyage, however,

acutely aware of his separation from Europe, the captain also regards himself and his companions as "wanderers on a prehistoric earth, on an earth that wore the aspect of an unknown planet" (p. 36). Here, in fact, having already lost the particularized support of comfortable navigational traditions (and their sanctions), the isolated Marlow now confronts the loss of significance within every articulation with which man has been associated. By moving beyond the trammels of Western civilization, beyond the beginning of historic time, he now arrives at the moment of creation and of infinite potential. As the elder Marlow suggests, he has reached the universe where "the mind of man is capable of anything—because everything is in it, all the past as well as all the future" (p. 37). It is at this point that the Marlow who has become upset with the company of lazy and self-indulgent pilgrims first begins to admire the inhabitants of the Congo, particularly the hardworking cannibals who in the face of hunger possess a baffling yet genuine self-restraint.

The cannibals may howl and leap and spin in the air, but they fascinate the impressionable Marlow precisely by virtue of the fact that in a world that seems devoid of any ostensible traditions they at least have provided themselves with effective sanctions for a manly conduct that is the antithesis of the pilgrims' mean and flabby behavior. Marlow may at first be uneasy about such fascination: "What thrilled you was just the thought of their humanity—like yours—the thought of your remote kinship with this wild and passionate uproar" (pp. 36–37). But finally, especially after the loss of his native helmsman, whose last look of "intimate profundity" he shall forever regard as a "claim of distant kinship" (p. 52), the captain acknowledges in himself a new moral discrimination and asserts new allegiance to such men of discipline. In a sense, perhaps, this new allegiance to discipline may merely serve the function of preserving the rapidly waning force of Marlow's tradition of sea discipline. On the other hand, the fact that Marlow responds so positively to the restrain  )f these cannibals who comfortably live in the prehistoric world of    )tentiality may reflect a new and broad appreciation for sea  anshir  s essentially the exercise of restraint within any world (preh  .toric    historic) of contingencies. Whatever the case, Marlow her  see·    ) be making an unlikely equation between the restraint of th   :ar     ils and that of the ancient navigators (remember that it is the ca   ·ⵏ    ·not the pilgrims, who help Marlow get the steamer

upriver),[8] which provides him with a new moral steadiness as he penetrates further into the Congo.

Despite this new allegiance to cannibals as "moral navigators," however, Marlow still has not reached the culmination of his critical journey into the prehistoric. For only with the end of the sixty-day journey at hand, and the steamer herself again "at her last gasp" (p. 39), does he become conscious that the special relief that he has anticipated as his moral salvation since leaving the Central Station is meaningless. As I indicated earlier, Marlow throughout his journey toward the Inner Station has regarded his steamer as "crawl[ing] toward Kurtz — exclusively" (p. 35). From the moment of his interview with the brickmaker, in fact, he has been "curious to see whether this man, who had come out equipped with moral ideas of some sort, would climb to the top after all, and how he would set about his work when there" (p. 31). During the darkest moments of the journey, therefore, the captain has comforted himself with the thought that Kurtz will soon provide him with an eloquent statement about life's meaning. Indeed, despite his demonstrable maturing and new allegiance to the cannibals, he has by virtue of relying upon Kurtz managed to avoid full absorption into the metaphysical subtleties of this prehistoric wilderness. Now, however, after the bewilderment of nearly sixty days of difficult navigating, he experiences a premonition of the futility not only of his own but also of Kurtz's verbalizing in a deaf and dumb wilderness:

> I fretted and fumed and took to arguing with myself whether or no I would talk openly with Kurtz; but before I could come to any conclusion it occurred to me that my speech or my silence, indeed any action of mine, would be a mere futility. What did it matter what any one knew or ignored? (P. 39)

This premonition, of course, leaves Marlow entirely vulnerable. Even if he has earlier had glimpses of the futility of articulating in the prehistoric, where all remains potential and thus unsanctioned, he has still anticipated from Kurtz a full definition of man's reality. In this moment, nevertheless, he finally knows deep within himself the essential futility of any articulation, whether prehistoric or historic. his point, therefore, having lost whatever limited sense of seamanship he may yet have retained from a previous era, he begins to embrace much broader

sense of "seamanship" (or authentic existence) that characterizes the cannibals' conduct.

Marlow's total vulnerability is evident not only in his realization but also in his navigational situation. About eight miles from the Inner Station he anchors for the night and the next morning discovers that the steamer is enshrouded in "a white fog, very warm and clammy, and more blinding than the night" (p. 40). By itself the fog offers little danger, but, accompanied by rather demoralizing cries and shrieks from natives whose intentions are not absolutely clear, the situation easily becomes a "most hopeless look-out." Because of the possibility of grounding the steamer, a cautious Marlow cannot immediately direct his steamer out of the terrifying situation. At the same time, however, the Central Station manager on the spot authorizes him "to take all the risks. . . . I refuse to take any" (p. 43). In this situation, obviously, the navigational tradition (here representative of Western civilization) has lost all its significance. In the same moment Marlow confronts both the impossibility of effective procedure and the specious warranting of any action he chooses. Such a nexus defines the final breakdown of the sanctions by which Marlow has organized his life and thus brings Marlow to the absolute nadir of his Congo experience.

It is true that when the fog lifts and the pilgrims begin their skirmish with the natives this captain does busy himself with directing the steamer through a narrow and suddenly very shallow passage along a series of islands. While he seems to be following procedure, however, he suddenly discovers that his helmsman has disrupted such procedure by leaving the wheel in order to help ward off the attackers. It is then, of course, that Marlow faces his most disconcerting moment in the Congo. For under attack, his steamer twisting off course, her bottom likely to rip on a rock or a snag, he faces the possibility of complete disaster and even death hundreds of miles away from further company support. At that moment, nevertheless, acting more instinctively than procedurally and thus in the manner of the natural navigators (that is, the cannibals), he grabs the wheel and becomes, himself, the active agent who unhesitatingly provides direction to his ship and her men. Bravely, while the smoke from the pilgrims' guns obscures his view of the ripple, he risks crowding the boat into shore where he by experience, at least if he had time to think about the situation, can expect deeper water. He is right. The boat does not hit bottom. At the same time that he handles the wheel, the native helmsman, wounded by a spear, falls to the floor, and

his blood seeps into Marlow's shoes.[9] Metaphorically, such seepage defines the moment of Marlow's death.

The implications of all these subtle details must now be made clear: (1) in the prehistoric Congo, a wilderness without the grace of moral sanctions, man faces a universe both of ultimate potentiality and of ultimate futility; (2) in this universe of purposelessness man, if he is to enjoy any sense at all of personal growth and fulfillment, must actively become his own helmsman and thus create personal, subjective sanctions for his own conduct; and (3) the assumption of such an active role even at the very best entails the death of the helmsman because he is asserting himself and his purposes against the stronger forces of the amorphous wilderness.[10] In the nadir of his Congo experience an assertive Marlow may save the steamer and become his own helmsman. Because of his identification with the cannibals, the natural seamen of the wilderness, he may even become conscious of himself (at least in contrast to the pilgrims) as the consummate navigator of the wilderness. At the same time, nevertheless, he shall never forget the significance of the native helmsman's last look of "intimate profundity" — a look that unites them in kinship and in "death." That look suggests that Marlow has realized what all sensitive men in Conrad's wilderness must realize: human achievement, no matter how creative and meaningful, remains a gesture of futility because such achievement rests on a heart not of eternal sanctions but of profound darkness.

The second bit of navigation, then, as I suggested in my introductory comments to this chapter, prompts in Marlow his most crucial maturation in the Congo. That such development has occurred becomes fully apparent in the third navigational situation, Marlow's pursuit of Kurtz in the jungle. Shortly after midnight following Kurtz's installment in a cabin of the steamer, Marlow suddenly glances into Kurtz's open cabin and discovers that he is gone. For the captain the moment is again, as when he discovers the desertion of his native pilot, disconcerting; he is "completely unnerved by a sheer blank fright, pure abstract terror" (p. 65). The shock is only momentary, nevertheless, for immediately Marlow gains the bank of the river, finds Kurtz's trail, and then — noting that Kurtz is crawling on all fours — exults in the discovery that he has the upper hand. Now, instead of struggling rather futilely with a caravan that does not understand him, or instead of despairing before the fundamental futility of all articulations, the captain pushes off into the jungle with a steadiness and assurance that surely underscore his recent achievement of a new perspective. At one point, despite being strangely "cocksure of everything," he may consider the possibility of becoming lost and thus remaining "alone and unarmed in the woods to an advanced age," but that possibility no longer upsets him. Instead, supported by his appreciation of the broad spaces and limitless time in the dark wilderness, he notes only that he has begun to confound "the beat of the [natives'] drum with the beating of [his] heart" and that he is "pleased at its calm regularity" (p. 66). The fact that the drums no longer confuse Marlow by itself may indicate the profound change in the captain's perspective. To be sure, there is the comment by the narrating Marlow that seems to demean this performance in overtaking Kurtz: "I was circumventing Kurtz as though it had been a boyish game" (p. 66). The suggestion that Marlow is participating in a game, however, merely accents the confidence that the captain feels as he navigates well, with the instinct of a cannibal who is comfortable in the wilderness, his rescue of the man with whom he has earlier, but especially now, identified himself.

Marlow's new and mature confidence also appears when, having overtaken Kurtz and recognized the danger from the natives if Kurtz should shout, he stuns Kurtz with the phrase, "You will be lost— utterly lost" (p. 67). The implication of the comment is that Kurtz is in danger of going beyond the pale, of being absorbed in an obsession in which he shall lose the existential choice to develop his own personal sanctions and subjective vision. When one recalls that Kurtz has "kicked himself loose of the earth" and that he has "kicked the very earth to pieces" in pursuing his obsession, one cannot but appreciate the magnitude of Marlow's achievement here. For if it is true that in a deaf and dumb wilderness there is no sanction to which the captain can appeal in order to terminate Kurtz's longing for complete assimilation among the natives, the captain must have enjoyed, as he says, a "flash of inspiration" or the maturity of genuine insight when he immediately zeroes in on the real issue. Years later, Marlow may tell his listeners that the conversation with Kurtz had "that terrific suggestiveness of words heard in dreams, of phrases spoken in nightmares" (p. 67), but if one recognizes that the captain's comment is rooted in his very recent appreciation of both the futility and the necessity of creative self-assertion amid the sights and the sounds and the smells of the wilderness, the comment can easily serve as a reflection of a matured Marlow's own superior insight and courage. The Marlow who brings Kurtz back to the steamboat is a Marlow who has achieved a perspective of the limits and yet the necessities of self-assertion far broader than any Kurtz has ever enjoyed. While Kurtz only in the final moments of his life, when he pronounces on the horror, recognizes both the corruption of his idealism and the fundamental emptiness of any articulation in the wilderness, the superior Marlow has already enjoyed such recognition before his arrival at the Inner Station.

The major difference that this new emphasis on Marlow's superiority to Kurtz entails is that the final section of the elder Marlow's narrative now reads as supremely ironic. For example, in the scene of Kurtz's illumination it appears as if the narrating Marlow is appreciating Kurtz's final perception as a consummate insight. After all, he suggests that there is a sudden change in Kurtz's features, "as though a veil had been rent" (p. 70), and thus that Kurtz is about to see the holiest of holies, the ultimate reality. Or he suggests that Kurtz is a "remarkable man" (p. 72) because he has had something to say when Marlow, if he were at the point of death, probably "would have nothing to say." Or he calls the final cry "an affirmation, a moral victory paid for by innumerable defeats, by abominable terrors, by abominable satisfactions" (p. 72). I do not wish, here, to accuse the elder Marlow of merely pulling red herrings across the texture of his narrative. And yet, while it is true that in the Congo—and beyond—this urbane captain appreciates the courage of Kurtz's final struggle, it is also true that the elder Marlow is, here, ironically minimizing the genius of his own illumination shortly before meeting Kurtz. Even if the elder Marlow should include other details that point to the steamer captain's inferiority of vision, details such as his increasing fever downriver or his restlessness in Brussels or his bewilderment before Kurtz's Intended, readers of this novel should not be deflected from the conviction that the captain has seen at least as much as Kurtz—and probably more because he has the opportunity to make his perception the basis of future action such as when he rescues Kurtz or lies to Kurtz's Intended. The Marlow who has suffered a profound weighting of perspective during his journey into the heart of the Congo may still need time to absorb all the implications of his insights, but there is no question that in this novel it is he who has achieved the superior vision.

The final section of *Heart of Darkness* is, then, a very subtle and ironic narrative that can be appreciated only on the basis of a firm understanding of Marlow's vocational dilemma at the beginning of his Congo experience and of his two moments of supreme realization, first when he arrives at the Central Station and then when he arrives at the Inner. Once the irony of the final section in Marlow's narrative is appreciated, however, one can avoid the recent unwarranted emphasis upon Kurtz's final struggle as the watershed that enables Marlow, after he is back in Brussels, to lie to the Intended. I do not want to take anything away from the dramatic importance of the death scene or the Brussels scene; clearly, they both have a profound impact upon the captain if only because they cause him great distress. But finally the reader must not misinterpret the nature of Marlow's silence at the end of the novel. The uneasy Marlow may for a long time remain silent about the significance, for him, of Kurtz's final struggle, but unless the reader recognizes that this silence, whether before the pilgrims or before Marlow's peers in Brussels, serves only as a measure of the captain's contempt for those who have not perceived the implications of living within a deaf and dumb universe, he may be too quick to overemphasize the supposed brilliance of Kurtz's final insight. Because it is not until the grace of future experience that is rooted in his philosophic upheaval in the Congo that Marlow begins to calm down and to consider seriously the possibility of relating its particular distresses to his saltwater friends, the captain's silence actually must be seen to possess its own brilliance. One can be sure, therefore, that when Marlow does relinquish his silence, he will not only adopt the same ironic, self-effacing tone that characterizes his subtle narrations of "Youth" and *Lord Jim*, but he will also acknowledge — for the discriminating listener and reader — the full significance of his Congo experience. It is in these terms, of course, that this captain's silence achieves its full eloquence.

# 6

# *Lord Jim* (I): Marlow's Interviews
# with Jim and with Jewel

Marlow's narrative in *Lord Jim* consists principally of a series of interviews with Jim, Brierly, Chester, the French lieutenant, Stein, Jewel,
and a number of minor figures such as the *Patna*'s delirious engineer or
the third-class deputy-assistant resident. Such emphasis upon interviews, as critics have been quick to note,[1] provides Conrad with shrewd
means for developing the literary impressionism with which his early
sea fiction is so frequently associated. Beyond this emphasis in *Lord
Jim* upon the impressionistic possibilities of narrative, however, the
novel also serves as an epistemological landmark in modern fiction for
the very reason that Marlow's act of recall in the several interviews is
essentially an effort to determine the truth about Jim's and especially his
own experience. The series of interviews, consequently, do not remain
isolated incidents in Marlow's consciousness but tend to converge toward, say, a definition of the type of heroism that Marlow regards as
necessary for existing in a modern world. Indeed, the one common de-
nominator of all the interviews is that they adumbrate the nature either
of Jim's or of Marlow's heroism. In this chapter, by examining the
interviews with Jim during the inquiry, then with Jim in Patusan, and
finally with Jewel in Patusan, I hope to provide a rich opportunity for
approaching the nature and the extent of the captain's growth as he
develops a new appreciation for the qualities of heroism appropriate to
modern existence.

It is Marlow's interview with Jim during the inquiry into Jim's desertion from the *Patna* that occasions the principal tension underlying this third, yet particularly fertile, period of growth. At the beginning of that interview, as a successful captain, Marlow indulges a mere whim in trying to understand what has happened to Jim. The whim, of course, smacks of smug superiority. The captain himself enjoys the security of genuine achievement. He thus knows that he must not palliate Jim's guilt by acknowledging his own weaknesses and failings, whether real or potential. By initially shunning any influence by which he might relieve some of Jim's distress, nevertheless, he actually reduces the interview to a one-sided affair that opens him to the accusation of complacent superiority: while Jim desperately tries to excuse his conduct during the *Patna* crisis by rehearsing several accounts of surprised innocence, Marlow keeps his own counsel or, at a maximum, indulges in ironic responses that he knows Jim will either not hear or fail to comprehend. Indeed, if Marlow does feel any sympathy for Jim, he generally disguises it in a posture of aloofness that he at the time regards as neutral observation. As shall be seen, however, such neutrality is hardly less than smug superiority.

It is true that before Jim's persistent badgering Marlow does suffer a steady loss of the cool confidence that belongs to his noncommittal pose. Jim's repetition of the argument of mere chance as the primary element in his desertion of the *Patna*, for example, ultimately brings the captain to the verge of anger: "I was aggrieved against him, as though he had cheated me — me! — of a splendid opportunity to keep up the illusion of my beginnings, as though he had robbed our common life of the last spark of its glamour" (p. 80). Such anxious rationalizations concerning chance, of course, deprive Marlow of the pride that he himself has painstakingly invested in successful achievement at sea. Beyond the personal issue, however, there is even a more critical issue at stake: because the captain knows that such rationalizations must finally entail the meaninglessness of all achievement, he here perceives himself in the delicate moral predicament of having to decide whether or not to relinquish his silence and to disabuse Jim of his precious notion. It is toward the end of Jim's account in the gallery of the Malabar, when Jim violently demands of Marlow, "What do *you* believe?" (p. 81), that the captain finally begins to face up to the possible deprivation of his neutrality. The moment is terrible, but in its terror, instead of exposing the weakness in Jim's stance, Marlow rather weakly succumbs to bewilderment: "Suddenly I felt myself overcome by a profound and hopeless fatigue, as though [Jim's] voice had startled me out of a dream of wandering through empty spaces whose immensity had harrassed my soul and exhausted my body" (p. 81). Such a perception, obviously enough, entirely vitiates any growing resolution in the captain to acquaint Jim with his folly. By choosing a path of lesser terror, moreover, Marlow here makes himself vulnerable to further recriminations.

Shaken from his smug superiority, Marlow now violates his earlier, seemingly well-reasoned stance of neutrality and accepts at least the vestige of a questionable responsibility for Jim by offering him money² so that he can disappear before the inquiry is complete. It is obvious that the captain has an interest in such a disappearance if it should help free him of his present moral predicament. Jim, however, refuses the offer, and at that point the captain must realize that he is inextricably caught up in the situation and shall not easily avoid further participation in Jim's affairs. "Provoked to brutality," he does decide to assert himself and to reveal his viewpoint, but then only discovers — ironically — that he cannot: "I opened my mouth to retort, and discovered suddenly that I'd lost all confidence in myself" (p. 94). Having earlier neglected or even repressed an explicit announcement of his own contempt for Jim's fabrication of a universe in which Jim is not guilty but only surprised, Marlow in effect must now labor under the continued suspension of his vision. Even if he has only now become fully conscious of the moral problems inherent both in Jim's "artful dodges to escape from the grim shadow of self-knowledge" and in his own dodges and self-deceptions, he cannot immediately recover his customary moral position except by abruptly terminating his relationship with this former mate who possesses no other friends. Such termination, however, is impossible. Indeed, because he is determined to be kind, Marlow quickly reconciles himself to the continuation of his disconcerting relationship with Jim — until Jim can manage on his own. Such a compromise, by its very nature, of course, must strike the reader as a full guarantee of further dismay and distress.

Marlow, to be sure, tries to justify his mistake of interfering in Jim's affairs by regarding Jim's problem as representative of a fundamental human predicament. By assisting Jim, he rationalizes, he is helping a man search for truth in a world where truth seems multiple and beyond human grasp. Such rationalizing, however, blurs two essential facts. First, the search for truth in a modern, Congo world is at the very least a task that each man enacts alone, in isolation. Marlow cannot in any way help another man achieve his truth. Second, while Marlow himself perceives an "Inconceivable" world in which man is "made to look at the convention that lurks in all truth and on the essential sincerity of falsehood" (p. 57), or in which all truth becomes a fiction, a convention, a verbalizing that cannot contain the delicate blends of light and darkness in human experience, Jim does not. The captain perceives man's experience in large epistemological and ontological terms; Jim, however, perceives such experience only in an immediate and very personal sense, that is, whether or not he himself has become the hero. When the captain overlooks the limitations in Jim's perspective and begins to direct Jim toward a larger apprehension of reality that shall serve as an "expiation for his [having craved] after more glamour than he could carry" (p. 92), therefore, the captain is virtually embarking upon the impossible. Because Jim imposes a very narrow and distinct condition (that he become the hero) upon his pursuit of truth, Marlow should not expect Jim to serve, except in a very limited way, as a paradigm for human experience. Only if Jim himself discovers the Inconceivable and its rejection of final truth, or only if he faces up to the inescapable uncertainties inherent in imperfect and incomplete perceptions, will he finally be able to deliver what Marlow expects of him. Such a radical transformation of perspective, however, would severely tax the credibility of the novel.

Marlow also justifies his interference in Jim's affairs on social grounds. Because he strongly believes that "there was nothing but myself between [Jim] and the dark ocean" (p. 106) of moral dissolution and even of suicide, he also hopes to provide the basic material assistance that will enable Jim to escape the disintegration of beggary and wandering. Such justification, however, smacks of Hollis's questionable rationalizations for assisting Karain. By providing Jim with the means to survive, Marlow may actually prevent the former mate from discovering for himself the fundamental dimensions of human articulation: that in a universe devoid of moral and spiritual sanctions every man must articulate, physically and verbally, primarily in order to stay alive and only secondarily in order to achieve a precious aspiration. On the *Patna*, of course, Jim is aware only of secondary articulation, and the consequence is terrible. Now, under the captain's sponsorship, he shall manage to retain the narrow attitudes and assumptions that promote his secondary pursuit of heroism, and again the result promises to be disastrous. As long as Marlow frees Jim of the stresses of seeking his own livelihood, Jim will avoid that necessary exposure to the world of the "Inconceivable" that alone is appropriate to the crisis at hand.

In *Lord Jim*, therefore, it is the captain, not Jim, who must tread the delicate and uncertain path of determining what is the proper course of action. It is he who must decide whether to assume some responsibility for Jim or to let him wander his own way. In the process of deciding he makes several critical mistakes. Already by interviewing Jim and by offering his assistance, he has become entangled in a situation that becomes increasingly more unbearable because he can do so little to alleviate Jim's distress. When he firmly directs the staggering Jim from the final scene in the courtroom into the Malabar Hotel, however, he finally acknowledges the full extent of his commitment to Jim that his earlier interest and interference may have foreshadowed: "If I had not edged him to the left here, or pulled him to the right there, I believe he would have gone straight before him in any direction till stopped by a wall or some other obstacle" (p. 104). Now fully involved in another man's fate, Marlow here begins to provide Jim with all sense of direction. While writing some letters of introduction, in fact, he makes the nature of their relationship absolutely definite: "I make myself unreservedly responsible for you" (p. 111). Such a statement, at least in the context of Conrad's early fiction of radical self-responsibility, probably defines the nadir of Marlow's dealings with Jim and, perhaps, of his own function as heroic paradigm at the core of that fiction. It also reveals how navigation in *Lord Jim*, with its great theme of human relationship, has become a matter not of reaching port but of striking the proper balance in dealing with people. Here, of course, Marlow is off balance.[3]

Months later, after assisting Jim through various employment with Denver, Egström, and De Jongh, Marlow still finds himself unable to construe the nature of the former mate's conduct—"whether his line of conduct amounted to shirking his ghost or to facing him out" (p. 119). After months of anticipating Jim's expiation, the problem before Marlow remains the same: whenever he tries to ascertain the quality of the young man's conduct, he himself becomes conscious only of the epistemological uncertainty that always seems to haunt him. As he tells his listeners, "I strained my mental eyesight only to discover that, as with the complexion of all our actions, the shade of difference was so delicate it was impossible to say" (p. 119) what Jim was doing with his ghost. To the very end of their relationship the subtle Marlow inhabits one world of vision and the reductive Jim another. Between the two there is virtually no communication, no paradigmatic equivalency. Nevertheless, even when the deplorable incident at Schomberg's in Bangkok clearly exposes the fact that Jim is in "retreat" (p. 121), the subtle Marlow still suspends his own moral viewpoint in order to retain contact with Jim. At that point he also provides a new justification (that of past involvement) for his conduct: "By that time I could not think of washing my hands of him" (p. 121). It is only on the passage away from Bangkok, when Marlow and Jim avoid speaking "for whole days," and when they "[don't] know what to do with [their] eyes" (p. 122), that the captain finally confronts the extreme differences between their perspectives and thus acknowledges to himself the folly of continued interference in Jim's life. Shortly thereafter, with Stein's support, he offers Jim the opportunity of entering Patusan and with the offer makes explicit what has become obfuscated during the course of their relationship: "I wished [Jim] to understand clearly that this [Patusan] arrangement, this — this — experiment, was his own doing: he was responsible for it and no one else" (p. 142). Such a statement, if only by virtue of its implications, contains for Marlow an important admission of past misjudgment. He has with good intentions meddled in Jim's affairs, yet now he rejects the false responsibility that has resulted perhaps in Jim's further demoralization and certainly in his own.

As the result of his first interview with Jim, then, Marlow awakens to the folly of ignoring — even in distressing human relationships — Conrad's primary ethic of self-responsibility. What Jim learns, if anything, as a result of the interview and the involvement with Marlow is more uncertain. After the conversation with Stein, Marlow does place the burden of responsibility for existing firmly in Jim's hands, but even then there is in Jim's exuberant acceptance of the opportunity (a response that makes the wisened Marlow "thoroughly sick" of him) a latent sense of relying upon Stein's past and especially upon his wonderful gift of a ring as the guarantees for his future in Patusan. At the point of separation, consequently, following months of his own bewilderment, Marlow can hardly avoid regarding Jim as being incorrigible as ever. What interests Marlow, therefore, and what gives his handling of the second interview in Patusan its focus, is whether Jim ever awakens to that "Inconceivable" world that alone can liberate Jim from his paralyzed pursuit of heroism. In my discussion of that interview (and of the novel's final fifty pages, which essentially grow out of that interview) I shall follow Marlow's lead and concentrate on the nature of Jim's pattern of awakening.

As a touchstone for this examination of Jim's awakenings in Patusan, it might be helpful to look at the wonderful comment on the act of awakening that Mircea Eliade includes in *Myth and Reality*. After pointing out that the overcoming of sleep is a typical initiatory ordeal, Eliade suggests that "not sleeping is not merely conquering physical fatigue but is above all a proof of spiritual strength. Remaining 'awake' means being fully conscious, being present in the world of spirit."[4] This comment, especially when juxtaposed to Elliott Gose's mythic analysis of Jim's Patusan experience,[5] seems to offer solid anthropological evidence for arguing that Jim in Patusan becomes the hero. After all, in Rajah Allang's stockade, and then in the ditch beyond the stockade, he not only refuses to resign himself to the weariness of mind and of body that his retreat from the sea has occasioned, but he distinctly conceives of himself as having awakened. Furthermore, after that escape from the Rajah and after his recovery in Doramin's house, he helps the Bugis defeat the forces of Sherif Ali and thus seems to achieve that "godhead" among the natives which Gose sees as the culmination of the heroic ordeal. Jim's success, however, is very deceiving, and when one closely examines Marlow's very subtle handling of metaphor in his account of the second interview with Jim, one can hardly avoid picking up the clues necessary for a new reading of Jim's Patusan experience.

It is while working upon a broken alarm clock during his imprisonment in Rajah Allang's stockade that Jim first becomes conscious of an awakening: "The true perception of his extreme peril dawned upon him" (p. 154). Jim may not know precisely what he will do, but he does recognize that his position in the stockade is unbearable and that he must act. In sharp contrast to his self-conscious paralysis during the *Patna* emergency, consequently, he in this instance embraces the necessity of the moment and executes his will almost as if courage to him were as natural as breathing:

> At once, without any mental process as it were, without any stir of emotion, he set about his escape as if executing a plan matured for a month. He walked off carelessly to give himself a good run, . . . went over "like a bird," and landed on the other side with a fall that jarred all his bones and seemed to split his head. (P. 155)

In addition to portraying a Jim who executes, not merely acts, this passage seems to equate the jarring of bones and the splitting of head with Jim's discovery of a new perspective for himself. In fact, if one is willing to accept the explosive impact of the fall upon Jim's head as metaphorically tantamount to the intrusion of new vision, this passage may serve as the basis for arguing that Jim has reached a turning point and is in this ordeal on the verge of becoming the hero.

As the narrative of the episode develops, however, Jim does not reveal the promise inherent in such an awakening. For in his flight away from the stockade he, instead of having become alive to new possibilities for approaching experience, continues a familiar yet dangerous tendency. As Marlow somewhat sardonically records, he "never thought of anything." Even when he runs, his perception of motion reflects only the sense of passivity: while running forward across the ground, he actually believes that "the earth seemed fairly to fly backwards under his feet." Then, when he leaps for the second time, this time across the creek, he lands in a soft mudbank and there discovers that he is firmly caught in the mud. By this point the subtle metaphoric implications within Marlow's handling of the interview have reached their first crescendo: the passivity that has characterized Jim's *Patna* behavior now fully defines his conduct in Patusan too. Even if, when trapped in the mud, Jim should believe that "he [comes] to himself," the reader can no longer overlook the considerable weight of other details that argue that he has not.

For those readers who still believe that this section of narrative supports the view that Jim has awakened, however, Marlow provides one further, very important clue. When he recounts how Jim desperately and furiously tries to claw his way out of the mudbank, he essentially continues the line of Jim's retreat: while clawing his way through the mud, Jim actually thrusts himself into a sensory imprisonment. As Marlow recounts: "Then he struck out madly, scattering the mud with his fists. It fell on his head, on his face, over his eyes, into his mouth" (p. 155). Here, by furiously attempting to overpower a threatening situation, Jim actually blinds himself and thus reverses the potential inherent in his initial awakening and the consequent leap from the stockade. Instead of having awakened into a perspective that would have enabled him to master this untoward situation, therefore, Jim has probably remained the victim of that perceptual paralysis that has defined all of his past re-

sponses to situations of emergency—whether on the training ship, on the *Patna*, or now in Patusan.

The fact that Jim has remained such a victim is even more evident in Marlow's continuation of the desperate struggle. For now, having blinded himself, Jim considers as his objective not the recovery of sight but the absolute destruction of the earth in which he has known only disappointment:

> He made efforts, tremendous sobbing, gasping efforts, efforts that seemed to burst his eyeballs in their sockets and make him blind, culminating into one mighty supreme effort in the darkness to crack the earth asunder, to throw it off his limbs. . . . (P. 155)

One may at first, of course, wish to regard this passage as testimony to Jim's new stature as hero. After all, while facing the imminence of death, he does seem to display a Herculean ("Samsonian" would be a better adjective) stature in his efforts to manage a bad situation when blind. Jim, however, is only a kid stuck in the mud, and his efforts now "to crack the earth asunder" belong to the exaggerations of a kid who has never matured beyond his world of make-believe. Instead of realistically attuning his perspective, even while blind, to the true nature of the difficulties that belong to this situation, Jim here, just as on the *Patna*, projects himself into a world of exaggerated dangers and difficulties and, consequently, ends up acting blindly and impulsively, with all of his strength, but with no sense of insight or understanding. The danger in the creek, to be sure, is very real, and thus he must act. The nature of his action, however, will remain very questionable until he develops a more realistic appraisal of his situation. Just as the young Marlow on the *Judea* becomes aware of the centuries-old context of seamanship and thus is able to face up to the long ordeal of the *Judea*'s final journey, or just as Marlow in the Congo becomes aware of the futility yet the necessity of human articulation and thus manages to survive the ravaging of the wilderness, so Jim might more realistically appraise this ordeal as a phenomenon that all men, not just heroes, must periodically face and endure. Such a perception at the very least would liberate him from that anxious heightening of response that ultimately reduces him to the unpredictability of impulse.[6]

Jim is not Marlow, however, and he does not enjoy such a liberation. In fact, conscious only of his exhaustion after having destroyed the

world that had threatened him, he does not even perceive himself as
hero when he finally climbs out of the mudbank. It is now, ironically,

> as a sort of happy thought[, that] the notion came to him that he
> would go to sleep. He will have it that he *did* actually go to sleep; that
> he slept—perhaps for a minute, perhaps for twenty seconds, or only
> for one second, but he recollects distinctly the violent convulsive start
> of awakening. (Pp. 155–56)

The revealing aspect of this passage, beyond the fact that Jim once more
wants to return to a passive state when circumstances require that he
stay awake, is that this moment is the third of a series: (1) the awakening
inside the stockade, (2) the coming to himself in the mudbank, and (3)
this convulsive start of awakening. That Marlow, having listened to
Jim's account of the episode, should set up Jim's experience in such
fashion is surely important. It is true that the series may serve as the
means by whicn Marlow stresses the fact that Jim has awakened, but it is
more likely, given the fact that the captain is thoroughly capable of such
subtlety, that he is exploring the series for its ironic possibilities. The
mere fact that Jim must awaken three times immediately suggests that he
is still prone to sleepiness and passivity. Furthermore, if one remembers
how this supposed hero stumbles into Doramin's camp, produces the
ring, and then goes to bed where he lies "like a log for I don't know how
long," one probably possesses the final bit of evidence necessary to
warrant the view that the metaphor of awakening in Marlow's rehearsal
of his Patusan interview with Jim is largely ironic.

That this ironic view of Jim's ordeal is plausible also becomes apparent upon reexamination of some of the other episodes in the Patusan
narrative. A good example is the incident in which Sherif Ali tries to
protect his territory from Jim's intrusion by sending his men to kill Jim.
Typically enough, Jim is sound asleep while the men wait for the oppor-
tune moment. Indeed, it is only because Jewel keeps watch that Jim
manages to awake to the danger: "Jim's slumbers were disturbed by a
dream of heavens like brass resounding with a great voice, which called
upon him to Awake! Awake! so loud that notwithstanding his desperate
determination to sleep on, he did wake up in reality" (p. 180). The very
fact that Jim needs to be awakened once more surely indicates that his
escape from the stockade has hardly changed him into a true hero. Beyond this basic fact, moreover, Jewel's awakening is no ordinary occur-
rence. Because it possesses overtones of resounding heavenly brass, its

very nature suggests that Marlow is again underscoring Jim's failure to make a genuine adjustment of perspective. The supporting details in the incident also point to the same failure. When Jim follows Jewel to the shed, for instance, it is she who directs the action because he is not "properly awake." Moments later, she is the one who puts the revolver into his hand and insists that the assassins are waiting in the shed. Then, when Jim becomes distressed because he finds in the shed only a heap of rags, it is she who steadily encourages him to defend himself. Obviously, Jewel, not Jim, is in command of the situation.

To be sure, the distraught Jim does discover the pair of eyes, and he does do the killing, but the metaphor once more betrays his weakness:

> He held his shot . . . deliberately. He held it for the tenth part of a second, for three strides of the man—an unconscionable time. He held it for the pleasure of saying to himself, that's a dead man! He was absolutely positive and certain. He let him come on because it did not matter. A dead man, anyhow. He noticed the dilated nostrils, the wide eyes, the intent, eager stillness of the face, and then he fired. The explosion in that confined space was stunning. (P. 183)

I have already noted in the episode of the mudbank Jim's passivity, then his desperate and impulsive attempt to escape, and finally his effort to "crack the earth asunder." In this passage there appears much the same type of metaphor: first a passive Jim; then a Jim who is desperate for "the relief of some reality, of something tangible" (p. 183), as an alternative to weeks of ill-defined danger; and finally a Jim who creates another explosion in his moment of self-assertion. In this episode he may not crack the earth asunder, but he does kill a man, and it is this killing that probably exposes him the most. For because the killing is a rather unnecessary act—unnecessary either because a Jim who acts quickly might have ordered all four of the men over the riverbank or because a gun-carrying Jim need never have resorted to the extreme (a head wound) when confronted with a knife—the killing becomes another of those impulsive deeds which at first glance may seem heroic but which finally accord only with Jim's confinement within his own egoism. By pulling the trigger, Jim again asserts himself—but only in a destructive fashion. In these terms, of course, the similarity between the episodes of the mudbank and the assassination becomes very striking.

There is beyond the narrative of Marlow's interview with Jim in Patusan (in the novel's concluding pages) one more episode of awakening. When Gentleman Brown arrives and threatens Jim's empire, Jim for at

least the third time finds himself trapped within foreboding circumstances. At the beginning of this instance, when confronted with Doramin's desire to kill Brown and his men, the Jim who has achieved an
apparent stature as hero and leader may proudly and comfortably
proclaim, "Everybody shall be safe," or "I am responsible for every
life in the land" (pp. 238, 240). Despite all his promises of security for
the whole population, however, and despite all his efforts to guarantee
Brown's return to the sea, he faces another rude awakening when the
villainous and uncontainable Brown finally heads downriver. For
Brown, unlike the natives who have been "taking [Jim's] word for anything and everything" (p. 163), does not acknowledge the power of
Jim's word and thus thinks nothing of violating the agreed-upon route.
The upshot is that Jim, lulled into sleep by his belief that with Brown's
departure he has once more earned the natives' trust, must endure
another awakening—first, to Tamb' Itam's news of the disaster downriver and, second, to a supposedly increased understanding:

> Then Jim understood. He had retreated from one world, for a small
> matter of an impulsive jump, and now the other, the work of his own
> hands, had fallen in ruins upon his head. . . . I [Marlow] believe that
> in that very moment he had decided to defy the disaster in the only
> way it occurred to him such a disaster could be defied. . . . The dark
> powers should not rob him twice of his peace. He sat like a stone
> figure. . . . It was then, I believe, he tried to write—to somebody—
> and gave it up. Loneliness was closing in on him. (P. 248)

This passage, one of the most crucial and yet one of the most misread in
the novel, is important metaphorically on at least three grounds.

First, Jim awakens for the last time in the novel, and again it is someone else, here Tamb' Itam, who awakens him. Second, he sits "like a
stone figure" while he considers the implications of this final disaster.
If one remembers Marlow's description of Jim during the *Patna* emergency, that Jim has turned into "cold stone from the soles of his feet to
the nape of his neck" (p. 59), one can even appreciate here the consistency in Marlow's characterization of Jim in both the *Patna* and the Patusan periods. A Jim who is incapable of dealing with a terrible
emergency among sleeping pilgrims is also finally incapable of dealing
with an extreme emergency even among natives whose trust he has
won. In both instances, when action and resolution become absolutely
necessary, he rather quickly resigns himself to the defeat of the moment
and thus singularly fails to grab on to the very crises out of which heroes

may arise. In both instances, a paralyzed Jim quits too soon. And third, Jim impulsively begins to write someone about the disaster but fails. Again, if one recalls Marlow's description of Jim's quiescence during the *Patna* emergency, that "it did not seem worthwhile to open his lips, to stir hand or foot," one can now understand why Jim consistently fails to turn the moment of emergency into a glorious opportunity for self-realization. On the training ship, then on the *Patna*, and finally in Patusan Jim discovers that he must articulate in a manner to which he is not accustomed or, more importantly, in which there is no guarantee of heroic justification. Unlike Marlow, who in the Congo fully embraces the necessity of action without the support of moral or heroic sanctions, Jim is never able to suspend himself or his pursuit of heroism long enough to discover the wonders even of that primary articulation of survival that possesses no immediate heroic quality. Indeed, because his character is so fixed in its dependence upon the accomplishment of heroic justification, he possesses only a limited range of responses to the contingencies of human existence. In this instance, for example, before what seems to him a whole world shattered, he loses all power of word and thus, instead of seizing the possibilities that belong even to this terrible moment, marches off to a virtual suicide.[7] Such a reaction can only delineate the fact that he has never enjoyed a meaningful awakening.

If Marlow's interview with Jim in Patusan establishes Jim as a fool, the interview with Jewel establishes the captain himself as the real hero of the novel. For in this interview, building upon what he has already discovered during his relationship with Jim a couple of years earlier, he achieves another moment of insight that is at least the equivalent of his perceptions during the second stage of navigation up the Congo River. This insight, in fact, is probably Marlow's most shrewd in the sense that it occurs on the very brink of suicide — when he must make the decision whether human existence, particularly his own, is worth the expenditure of any more effort. Obviously, although his affirmative decision may then seem rather weak or even anticlimactic, such a harrowing moment shall nicely serve as the keystone for an appreciation of Marlow as Conrad's major paradigm for handling modern experience.

The interview with Jewel is markedly similar to Marlow's bewildering interview with Jim during the inquiry. Just as Jim then bitterly decries the world of chance and, in doing so, exposes the captain to the perplexity of perceiving the "Inconceivable," so Jewel denounces the

uncertainties of Jim's love for her and, while citing as proof for her concern Cornelius's cruelty toward her mother, momentarily deprives the
sensitive Marlow of all his usual composure:

> [Jewel's account] had the power to drive me out of my conception of
> existence, out of that shelter each of us makes for himself to creep
> under in moments of danger, as a tortoise withdraws within its shell.
> For a moment I had a view of a world that seemed to wear a vast and
> dismal aspect of disorder, while, in truth, thanks to our unwearied ef-
> forts, it is as sunny an arrangement of small conveniences as the mind
> of man can conceive. But still — it was only a moment: I went back
> into my shell directly. One *must* — don't you know? (P. 190)

Marlow may be wiser about the dangers of "meddling" following the
awkward conclusion to his earlier relationship with Jim, and yet here he
ignores such past distress and allows himself to become entangled with
Jewel in another relationship that again, no matter how brief, shall
prove disastrous. The fact that Marlow is so generous with himself, of
course, is very important, for it argues that at his mature age and even
after earlier disappointments this sensitive captain regards as necessary
his attempts to understand and assist in another's difficulties. The Marlow who has dealt with Jim knows that men are responsible only for
themselves; he knows that loneliness is "a hard and absolute condition
of existence" or that "it is when we try to grapple with another man's
intimate need that we perceive how incomprehensible, wavering, and
misty are the beings that share with us the sight of the stars and the
warmth of the sun" (p. 109). Such knowledge, however, does not prevent the captain from listening attentively to Jewel's distress. Even if
such listening momentarily forces him out of his shell, or even if he
again perceives, as in the Congo or in his first interview with Jim, the
confusion and the disorder that underlie the sunny and sometimes mad
arrangement of words and conveniences in which all men shelter themselves, or, finally, even if he discovers, when Jewel's account reaches
its climax, the loss of "the familiar landmarks of emotion" and thus becomes conscious of falling over the edge of the earth as the ground
"melts" under his feet, he continues to sustain himself in his effort with
the hope that at least his concern will reduce her strain.

The problem in the interview, nevertheless, just as in Marlow's first
interview with Jim, is that Jewel is wrestling with a ghost and demands
that Marlow assist her in such an impossible task. She wants from
Marlow absolute confirmation that Jim, unlike Cornelius, will remain

true to his love. The captain, in turn, largely because he is fully experienced in the dangers of becoming involved in such a task, immediately recognizes the inadequacy of any reply he might offer to such a plea. As he later informs his listeners, "for such a desperate encounter [he needed] an enchanted and poisoned shaft dipped in a lie too subtle to be found on earth" (p. 192).[8] He, therefore, even though he wants to assist the bewildered girl, for a time tries to avoid further involvement and becomes very reluctant to provide even superficial encouragement or assurance. In this instance, of course, in contrast to his dealings with Jim, Marlow cannot ease himself into involvement by providing material assistance. What Jewel needs is moral, not material, support, and if the captain is to help her, he must turn at once to an utterance of moral significance that commits him to her in a fashion even more definitive than the offer to Jim of a letter of introduction. To the extent, then, that this supremely wise Marlow becomes involved despite his knowledge that no moral utterance can possibly satisfy her, he is already well on his way toward becoming a meddler for the second time in the novel.

At first Marlow tries to persuade Jewel that Jim will never leave Patusan by expressing a simple statement and a painful truth that he himself has trouble acknowledging: "In the whole world there was no one who ever would need his heart, his mind, his hand" (p. 193). From a cosmic perspective, the perspective in which loneliness is "a hard and absolute condition," Marlow is surely right. From an immediate perspective, from the doubting Jewel's, he is wrong. Jewel and Patusan need Jim — of that she is certain. Marlow, however, even though he may appreciate the truth of her perspective, maintains his larger angle of vision, and when Jewel flatly rejects his first truth, he brutally announces another cosmic truth — that Jim "is not good enough" (p. 194). Indeed, shocked by Jewel's violent reaction to this second truth, "You lie!" he further underscores his own attachment to the cosmic perspective by lamely muttering, "Nobody, nobody is good enough." Jewel, understandably enough, ignores such muttering as completely incomprehensible. She continues to suffer, and now before the disquieting ineffectuality of his efforts to assist her, Marlow, too, begins to suffer. At the very least, he now faces the necessity of acknowledging the limitations within his own, supposedly superior, cosmic perspective. Indeed, because his truths are true only for himself and not for Jewel, he now recognizes for the first time, whether in his dealings with Jim or with Jewel, the absolute futility of all his solipsistic concern—both in the past and in the present. The upshot is that he suddenly feels that he "had done nothing" at all to help Jewel. At this point, clearly enough, the interview turns into a rout: having failed to help Jewel even after compromising himself by meddling, he now bitterly queries himself, "What was the use?"

In *Lord Jim* this query signals the moment not only of Marlow's retreat from the interview with Jewel but also of his complete capitulation to man's pitiable dilemma. For having observed his wisdom fail to register any appreciable difference in the lives of both Jim and Jewel, he now becomes aware of the essential truth that although men may establish relationships in order to exert some influence upon the direction of their fate, these relationships cannot develop beyond the inescapable solipsism that permeates and thus isolates all perspectives, and furthermore, that without the possibility of full communication or of absolute relationships, contingency — and perhaps futility — becomes the fundamental condition of all human experience. In the interview with Jim during the inquiry, Marlow may have become aware of the folly of obfuscating the ethic of self-responsibility. In the interview with Jewel, however, he absorbs the much more sobering fact that chance and fate rule the cosmos. As he tells his listeners, "It is not Justice the servant of men, but accident, hazard, Fortune — the ally of patient Time — that holds an even and scrupulous balance" (p. 194) in human existence. Such a cold comment, nevertheless, is rather tame. At the time that Marlow is absorbing this truth, he is also conscious of perceiving the universe as a much more "sinister reality" that victimizes all men: "It was as though I had been shown the working of the implacable destiny of which we are the victims — and the tools" (p. 195). Even though he has already faced the horrors of the Congo, Marlow with this perception now approaches the absolute nadir of all his experience.[9]

As Marlow flees the disquieting interview with Jewel, he stumbles across the solitary grave of Jewel's mother and there, partially because the mother's weeping death has served as the occasion for Jewel's distress, finds his attention fully arrested. There, in fact, in a "mournful, eclipse-like light," he notices that the blossoms possess unusual shapes, as though "destined for the use of the dead alone," that the white coral around the grave gleams "like a chaplet of bleached skulls," and that the silence seems deathlike: "Everything around was so quiet that when I stood still all sound and all movements in the world seemed to come to an end" (p. 196). At first, of course, it may appear that Marlow, despite his retreat, has merely failed to escape the occasion for the bewildering interview with Jewel. By this point, however, the imagery and the suggestions of death essentially underscore the fact not of Jewel's mother's weeping death, but of Marlow's own ''death'' as a result of his discovery of all men as solipsists and thus as ineffectual victims of fate. In this moment before the grave, this wisest of Conrad's early heroes may actually be considering whether to capitulate to the futility of all human action. In the silence he certainly perceives the whole earth as the scene principally of death:

> It was a great peace, as if the earth had been one grave, and for a time I stood there thinking mostly of the living who, buried in remote places out of the knowledge of mankind, still are fated to share in its tragic or grotesque miseries. In its noble struggles, too — who knows? The human heart is vast enough to contain all the world. It is valiant enough to bear the burden, but where is the courage that would cast it off? (P. 196)

Marlow knows that the solipsist, who is everyman, owns the heart ''vast enough to contain all the world,'' that he participates in both the ''tragic or grotesque miseries'' and the ''noble struggles,'' and also that he does not have the ''courage that would cast [the burden of such futile participation] off.'' In this one moment of fully realizing the solipsistic horror of man's pitiable dilemma, however, Marlow himself probably flirts with the possibility of casting off the intolerable burden of futility. He has reached the point of moral, if not of physical, suicide.[10]

The captain, nevertheless, does not die. The next day, when he returns to the sea never to visit Jim again, he leaves behind all suggestion of the grave and accepts with new vigor the life that only a few hours earlier had appalled him: ''Freshness enveloped us, filled our lungs, quickened our thoughts, our blood'' (p. 201). Tingling with enthusiasm, and once more surveying the vast horizon of the sea as if his heart does indeed contain the world, Marlow is ''like a man released from bonds who stretches his cramped limbs, runs, leaps, responds to the inspiring elation of freedom. 'This is glorious!' '' (p. 201). Such a drastic change in Marlow's attitude may seem abrupt, but there is good justification for it in the simple fact that no man, unless he embraces bitterness or turns mad, can long endure the focus upon life's horror. In the interview with Jewel, Marlow has penetrated to the heart of human experience and to the essential futility of all action and relationship. Having fled the interview, however, and having struggled with despair at the gravesite, he recovers a balance of perspectives. With the dawn of a new day he knows deep within himself that the cosmic perspective, for which he has a penchant, can reduce all human endeavor to futility. At the same time he also appreciates how an immediate perspective enlarges that same endeavor to the significance of tragedy or joy. With his return to the sea, then, he recovers the immediacy of perspective that he had surrendered upon his penetration into the Patusan jungle and thus now exuberantly delights in the glorious possibilities of navigation before him.

Marlow's movement from a posture of smug superiority and cosmic forbearance while meddling in Jim's and Jewel's affairs to that of exuberant delight in a perspective of immediacy upon his return to the sea thus constitutes a new critical basis for understanding the nature and the magnitude of Marlow's self-realization in *Lord Jim*. At the very least, this sensitive captain with his strong inclination toward the cosmic has discovered the necessity for becoming even more flexible as he grows older. Hereafter, therefore, instead of an exaggerated allegiance either to a cosmic or to an immediate perspective, he might be expected to display a more effective balance of the two. In this sense, of course, *Lord Jim* becomes a tribute not to Jim, whose pattern of awakening is never genuine, but to Marlow himself. The captain knows that in his dealings with Jim and Jewel it is he who has truly awakened, and for that reason his Patusan visit, the occasion for perhaps his greatest illumination, "remains in the memory motionless, unfaded, with its life arrested, in an unchanging light" (p. 200).

Because Marlow's memory of his Patusan visit does remain undimmed, he cannot in later years avoid relating it to his friends. Indeed, before them he musters his greatest narrative powers in an attempt to recover the precise quality of that spectacular maturation that he has enjoyed in middle age. When he as narrator finishes his account approximately fifty pages before the actual end of the novel, consequently, he hardly regards the tale as "incomplete" (p. 205), as does the unidentified listener. In his narrative account this wise and very subtle captain has fully detailed that process of seasoning that has brought him to the very brink of suicide but that finally culminates in the exuberance of the next morning. *Lord Jim* as Marlow's tale and as a tale of maturation ends then.[11] The remaining fifty pages, as has already been seen, merely disclose Jim's fate, a suicide, which is the full extension of his retreat from any significant awakening. Jim's story is an important dimension of *Lord Jim* if only because it provides the occasion for Marlow's growth, but the fact that Marlow believes it necessary to share Jim's fate only with the unidentified listener by itself tends to indicate that the real story is Marlow's — and the real end Marlow's return to the sea and the balancing of perspectives.

# 7

## *Lord Jim* (II): Marlow's Interviews with the Lieutenant and with the Philosopher

In the light of the prevalent irony within Marlow's handling of Jim's pattern of apparent awakening, Marlow's interviews with the French lieutenant and with Stein beg for reexamination. For while the comments and characters of both the lieutenant and Stein have frequently served as critical bases for interpreting the novel,[1] their customary stature may not endure much scrutiny if one focuses attention not upon theme, as most critics have done, but upon the ambiguous quality of the narrative in their interviews. The two interviews are, of course, vastly different. By juxtaposing the two interviews in the light of Marlow's shrewd perceptions of himself (as outlined in the previous chapter), nevertheless, it may be possible to develop new views of these two men and thus an even fuller and more subtle appreciation of Marlow's narrative method and insight.

In Marlow's interview with the French lieutenant, it might be wise to isolate first one of those passages in which Marlow seems to underscore the shrewd insight of this French officer. Consider, for example, this statement: "[The officer's] imperturbable and mature calmness was that of an expert in possession of the facts, and to whom one's perplexities are mere child's-play'' (p. 89). Such a statement has probably prompted most readers of the novel to regard this lieutenant as an oracle of as much insight as possessed by the seemingly wise Stein, and yet in the statement there is the possibility of another interpretation. The sentence that precedes the statement reads: ''I felt *as though* I were taking professional opinion on the case'' (emphasis added). On the surface the prefatory comment, too, many tend to underscore a flattering view of the Frenchman, but if one recognizes that the conditional conjunction *as though* may also imply that Marlow is *not necessarily* taking professional opinion on Jim's case, one may have reason to conclude that Marlow is here tantalizing his listeners with a red herring. Moreover, the fact that Marlow virtually concludes the heart of the lieutenant's analysis of fear and cowardice with another such construction probably indicates that some hesitation is warranted. The lieutenant himself may insist that his views on fear are ''absolutely so'' because ''at my age one knows what one is talking about,'' but Marlow counters such insistence by pointing out that the officer has ''delivered himself of all this as immovably *as though* he had been the mouthpiece of abstract wisdom'' (p. 89; emphasis added). Again the conditional nature of the statement arouses suspicion, and finally, recognizing that Marlow carefully frames his rehearsal of the lieutenant's commentary on fear with similar constructions, the reader does well to guard himself against superficial acceptance of this French officer as a vehicle for Conrad's best insight.

The need for caution becomes more apparent if one considers the very real problem facing the narrating Marlow: unless he is to acknowledge his own attitudes very explicitly (an approach that would violate the prevailing ambiguity in his other interviews), how is he to maintain his distance from this lieutenant who seems so shrewd but who finally offers little, if any, insight into the matter of Jim's desertion? Marlow solves the problem early in the interview by emphasizing the lieutenant's appearance, that he is a ''quiet, massive chap . . . sitting drowsily'' over a drink, with shoulder-straps ''a bit tarnished'' and clean-shaved cheeks that are ''large and sallow'' (p. 84). Here, in the officer's substantial physique there is at least a suggestion of weariness and decay, perhaps even a hint of an ineffectuality that has prevented him from really ''getting on'' in his profession at sea. In succeeding passages Marlow is quick to reaffirm the lieutenant's ''ponderous immobility'' of body, the ''dispassionate'' movement of his eyebrows, the ''inert attitude'' of his posture, the ''placid expression of his face,'' and the passionless and machine-like phraseology of his speech—in general, the "torpid demeanour" of his being.[2] It is true that Marlow may at one point suggest that the officer's immobility "had that mysterious, almost miraculous, power of producing striking effects by means impossible of detection which is the last word of the highest art" (p. 86), but there one should not be fooled. Even if the lieutenant possesses such power, or even if he possesses two scars from gunshot and saber wounds that tend to attest to his character as hero, one's sense of his stolid appearance— at least as filtered through Marlow's eyes—must be that he has resigned himself to a conservative life of self-preservation that probably guarantees the fact that he, in contrast to Marlow, shall never rise higher than being "third lieutenant of the *Victorieuse*" (surely in this context an ironic name). Marlow's initial solution to his narrative problem, however, given the reader's strong predilection to trust the lieutenant, is not enough.

Beyond providing a series of descriptive details as clues to the nature of the lieutenant's being, Marlow is also generous in his use of proleptic simile. When Marlow first describes the lieutenant, for example, he concludes that the officer "looked like a man who would be given to taking snuff" (p. 84). Such a habit need not be unsavory, but the implication that the habit is distasteful—and thus reflects disadvantageously to the lieutenant—is nonetheless apparent in the conditional tone of the observation. That use of simile, however, is virtually harmless when compared to the second, the one in which Marlow unmistakably qualifies the officer's appearance and thus serves warning upon his listeners to be careful about their responses to his narration:

> He looked [*like*] *a reliable officer,* no longer very active, and he was seamanlike, too, in a way, though as he sat there, with his thick fingers clasped lightly on his stomach, he reminded you of *one of those snuffy, quiet village priests,* into whose ears are poured the sins, the sufferings, the remorse of peasant generations, on whose faces the placid and simple expression is *like a veil* thrown over the mystery of pain and distress. (P. 85; emphasis added)

Here, with the two similes and the metaphor of the snuffy village priest, Marlow delicately questions the officer's reliability or seamanship and especially his insight. The fact that the expression on his face may merely be a veil is a particularly damaging suggestion, and it points toward the later use of another simile that surely reveals all: the lieutenant is "as incapable of an emotional display as a sack of meal" (p. 86).

By now, having observed that Marlow develops narrative distance by virtue of the ambiguities inherent in both descriptive and figurative language, the reader is well prepared to interpret the performance of this Frenchman who is proud of his conduct during the *Patna* crisis. At the beginning of the interview, after it has by chance become apparent that the two men have a bond in the *Patna* affair, the lieutenant assumes before Marlow an air of "philosophic indulgence" and "resignation" (p. 85) as he recounts, first, the potential explosiveness of the scene around the corpse lying on the bridge of the *Patna* and, second, the necessity of his staying aboard the steamer while she is being towed by the French gunboat. Such an air can smack of a justifiable pride in his faithful attention to hazardous duty, but already at this stage of the interview, given Marlow's ambiguities and the lieutenant's "stolid glibness," the reader can hardly avoid concluding that the air smacks more of superiority than of justifiable pride. The lieutenant knows that, in contrast to the *Patna*'s officers, he has lived "up to the mark" and, having done so, now appears the soul of honor. From the beginning of the interview, therefore, this rather smug lieutenant expects to hold the upper hand and to indulge himself in a full and self-gratifying discussion of his participation in the crisis. The rehearsing of the crisis promises him at the very least a sense of unquestionable self-validation. Even when he finishes his recollections of the crisis and listens to Marlow's introduction of new facts on the matter, he continues to content himself with such smug and knowing punctuations as "*Parbleu!*" or "Ah, bah!" or "Very interesting!" or "*Eh bien!*" Never does he relinquish his hold upon a self-image of unmistakable superiority, and thus the reader—with Marlow—can only conclude that his involvement in the interview is essentially a self-serving act.

Marlow himself shrewdly acknowledges his awareness of the lieutenant's self-serving performance when he several times, in the latter half of the interview, exposes the officer's careful posturing of responses. For example, he suggests that the lieutenant, having finished his account of the crisis, yet waiting for Marlow's development of new facts, "suddenly, but not abruptly, *as if the appointed time had arrived* for his moderate and husky voice to come out of his immobility, . . . pronounced, '*Mon Dieu!* how the time passes!' " (p. 87; initial emphasis added). Once more, with the introduction of a conditional clause, one faces a narrative key precisely designed to expose the lieutenant's manipulation of a veil. Much in the same manner, when Marlow does begin his rehearsal of the new facts ("There were living men, too"), the lieutenant agrees half audibly and, "*as if* after mature consideration" (p. 88; emphasis added), murmurs, "Evidently." Some minutes later, when Marlow finishes his account, the officer lamely responds, "very interesting," but then adds, "*as if* speaking to himself, 'That's it. That *is* it!' " (p. 88; initial emphasis added). Even at the end of the interview, when the two men are suddenly quiet, the conditional still intrudes into the narrative: "I sat silent, and he too, *as if* nothing could please him better" (p. 90; emphasis added). The point of this emphatic use of the conditional is delicate but very crucial: throughout the interview, especially at the moments when the lieutenant may appear at his most perceptive or oracular, Marlow recognizes in him a self-consciousness that instead of supporting an appearance of wisdom, actually convicts the officer of engaging in a very deliberate performance. This officer is no villain—at least he is not trying to manipulate Marlow to the captain's disadvantage—but he is giving himself, perhaps without fully realizing it, the airs of a superior wisdom and insight that the nature of his character cannot support.

The presence of a performance, then, becomes the key to interpreting the lieutenant's remarks. Just as the lieutenant has managed to appear "profoundly responsive" with his many soft and knowing punctuations, so now, in contrast to the hesitant Marlow, he easily provides Jim's case with a bold philosophic commentary that the captain himself, upon first hearing it, accepts as definitive "professional opinion." Several times the officer launches the sweeping generalization that "one is always afraid"; or that "the fear, the fear—look you—is always there"; or that "at the end of the reckoning one is no cleverer than the next man—and no more brave" (p. 89). The words on the surface seem profound, rooted in the wisdom of experience, and the reader—like Marlow—may at first want to regard them as a shrewd professional estimation of Jim's behavior. Finally, however, because the generalizations do not apply *specifically* to the dilemma that Jim faces upon the *Patna*, they are of little more value than the knowing punctuations that have preceded them. In fact, because they do not take into account the particulars of the emotional confusion that Jim experiences upon the *Patna*'s collision with the derelict, the generalizations mirror only the character of the lieutenant's own timid being. As such a reflection, they cannot in any way serve as genuine keys to understanding Jim's—or anyone else's—fear and cowardice, and thus they are, at least in this narrative texture, nothing more than further red herrings designed to keep the reader wary and fully attentive to the novel's principal focus upon the nature of Marlow's own growth.

For substantiation of this negative view of the lieutenant's generalizations, one need turn only to the climax of his sweeping discussion of fear. There, after suggesting that ''there is somewhere a point'' (p. 89) where every man will crumble in fear, the officer keys on the one generalization that is at the root of all his commentary. It is the generalization by which he has organized all his personal experience, and he confidently offers it up as the ultimate expression of his wisdom and insight: the brave man wards off the possibility of crumbling before fear by creating for himself a tight pattern of responsible conduct. This relationship between fear and habit he makes very definite:

> Man is born a coward (*L'homme est né poltron*). It is a difficulty— *parbleu*! It would be too easy otherwise. But habit—habit—necessity —do you see?—the eye of others—*voilà*. One puts up with [fear]. And then the example of others who are no better than yourself, and yet make good countenance. (P. 90)[3]

Because of the emotional conviction with which this comment is invested, it is abundantly clear that the lieutenant himself relies upon habit and social pressure in order to deal with fear. For him ''habit'' and ''the eye of others'' possess only positive overtones. The very fact that he does not perceive the limitation of potential that such devotion to routine or to public approval may entail, however, argues that he does not, perhaps cannot, see beyond the rigid texture of generalizations within which he has developed his life. This officer is not particularly imaginative, and ultimately his commentary on cowardice is instructive not for its insight into Jim's case but for its exposure of his own folly.

The French lieutenant, then, is a figure in the novel who cannot serve as a positive standard of judgment against which to measure Jim's failure. Because he has based his existence upon the avoidance of those fears and tensions that provoke new exertions and thus new self-discoveries and achievements, he possesses little genuine vitality—whether physical or imaginative. He may proclaim his vision as truth, but the reader knows that his assurance reflects only his utter insulation within a routine that actually deadens his interest in other people and their problems. Marlow himself fully prepares the reader for such a final judgment of this officer when he announces, immediately before reciting

Jim's problems on the *Patna*, that he has had a moment of vision (this announcement is Marlow at his most explicit):

> I raised my eyes when he spoke, and I saw him *as though* I had never seen him before. I saw his chin sunk on his breast, the clumsy folds of his coat, his clasped hands, his motionless pose, so curiously suggestive of his having been simply left there. Time had passed indeed: it had overtaken him and gone ahead. It had left him hopelessly behind with a few poor gifts: the iron-grey hair, the heavy fatigue of the tanned face, two scars, a pair of tarnished shoulder-straps. . . . (P. 87; emphasis added)

Once more the captain resorts to the conditional, and again the conditional refers the reader not merely to a hypothesis but to an essential truth. Here, in fact, the lieutenant's weariness and ineffectuality, which were merely hinted at near the beginning of the interview, become genuine fact. A short time later, when Marlow finishes his recital of Jim's history, he notes in another moment of vision an even further degeneration in the lieutenant: "His chin seemed to sink lower on his breast, his body to weigh heavier on his seat. . . . a sort of preparatory tremor passed over his whole person, as a faint ripple may be seen upon stagnant water even before the wind is felt" (p. 88). The simile of stagnant water is particularly revealing, and it leads to a final moment of vision when, at the point of beginning his meaningless discourse on fear and cowardice, the officer grabs his drink and awakens Marlow to the fact that "the three last fingers of his wounded hand were stiff and could not move independently of each other, so that he took up his tumbler with an ungainly clutch" (p. 89). If in earlier references to the officer's wounds there was a hint of heroism, that hint now fails before these suggestions of stagnation and stiffness.

Finally, of course, these moments of vision, by providing the reader with further support for rejecting the lieutenant's commentary, become the basis for the reader's reaction to the conclusion of the interview. For then, when a mistaken Marlow assigns to this officer a lenient view of Jim's affair, the captain first notes how the stiff lieutenant "[draws] up his heavy eyelids" and then comments:

> Drew up, I say—no other expression can describe *the steady deliberation of the act*—and at last [he] was disclosed completely to me. I was confronted by two narrow grey circlets, *like two tiny steel rings* around the profound blackness of the pupils. The sharp glance, coming from that massive body, gave a notion of extreme efficiency, *like a razor-edge* on a battle-axe. (P. 90; emphasis added)

On the surface the two similes, with their overtones of steeliness and efficiency, may even yet, if the reader is not careful, evoke sympathy for the lieutenant. At the same time, however, the reader cannot ignore the fact that this moment provides Marlow with his fullest insight into the character of this lieutenant who even at the end of the interview is relying upon a veil or the appearance of perspicacity and efficiency as his credential of wisdom. It is now, therefore, when the lieutenant abruptly cuts off Marlow's lengthy but precise commentary upon Jim's dilemma, that the captain experiences the complete deflation of his earlier expectations. For in this moment the Frenchman, getting up on his feet "with a ponderous impetuosity, as a startled ox might scramble up from the grass," thoroughly reduces his supposed insight to a heavy and mindless repetition of the necessity of honor: "But the honour—the honour, monsieur!... The honour... that is real—that is! And what life may be worth when...when the honour is gone...I can offer no opinion. I can offer no opinion—because—monsieur—I know nothing of it" (p. 90). Here the lieutenant's stupidity becomes inescapable. He may think he understands honor, but in reality he is nothing more than a dull yet determined ox who faces up to his inadequacy only at the very end of the interview when he acknowledges to Marlow, "This, monsieur, is too fine for me—much above me—I don't think about it" (p. 91). According to Marlow, such a revelation merely puts the "blight of futility" on the interview. It is clear, however, that the essential blight is in the Frenchman himself.

The interview between Marlow and Stein is even more confusing. At least in the narrative of the lieutenant's interview the weight of the evidence, while disguised in Marlow's ambiguities, unquestionably gathers against this officer as a figure of insight or as a wise commentator on Jim's dilemma.[4] With Stein, however, the evidence does not all go one way. Because Marlow continues to appreciate his friendship with Stein even after the interview is over, one can only hope to discover in Marlow's use of metaphor and irony a pattern of shifting attitudes toward the philosopher. Total diminishing of character and vision, as with the French lieutenant, is impossible. In a sense, therefore, narrative ambivalence becomes the critical touchstone for the whole interview with Stein.

It is when Marlow recounts how Stein removes himself from Celebes following the deaths of his friend Mohammed Bonso and the members of his own family that one's admiration for this philosopher first requires some major qualification.[5] Marlow himself comments upon that removal by pointing out that Stein has become, after amassing a considerable fortune, very solitary and—if not misanthropic—for the most part devoted to classifying the dead specimens of his collections. Even if there is no explicit criticism in such a remark, the comment does suggest that there has been a severe diminishing of spirit: Stein's joy as a young trader in Celebes has turned to somber gloom. There is in the text one image, the image of the butterfly, that particularly supports the fact of this diminishing.

On the day of his attempted assassination, a day in which he is fully aware of his good fortune in possessing friends and family and the marvels of adventure, Stein catches the rare butterfly about which he even years later is so proud: "When I opened these beautiful wings and made sure what a rare and so extraordinary perfect specimen I had, my head went round and my legs became so weak with emotion that I had to sit on the ground" (p. 128). This image of a live butterfly that has landed upon a heap of dirt obviously contrasts sharply with the catacombs of *Coleoptera* that presently surround Stein in his well-organized study. The prize butterfly is itself now dead, and the implication is that its death is a metaphor for Stein's own life: just as he kills the beautiful butterfly and prizes it within his collections, so with his own removal from Celebes he destroys the vitality of his life in the wilderness and now prizes it, even idealizes it, by restraining himself from further active involvement in human affairs. Instead of actively engaging in the turmoils of present sorrows and joys, he is content in his middle-aged solitude merely to indulge himself with the memories of past happiness. By exchanging his status as a prize butterfly fluttering over a clean earth for that of a butterfly pinned to its tray, therefore, Stein has essentially tried to make his experience in Celebes altogether sufficient for the remainder of his life.[6]

It is true, nevertheless, that even in death the butterfly retains its beauty. Listen for a moment to the expert collector himself discourse in an excited, somewhat staccato manner about the prize he has caught years in the past:

Look! The beauty—but that is nothing—look at the accuracy, the harmony. And so fragile! And so strong! And so exact! This is Nature—the balance of colossal forces. Every star is so—and every blade of

grass stands so—and the mighty Kosmos in perfect equilibrium produces—this. This wonder; this masterpiece of Nature—the great artist. (P. 126)

The terms of the comment are very revealing. When Stein removes
himself from the jungle of Celebes and its insecurity, he fashions for
himself a life of solitude that protects him from the uncertainties of
human contact. The upshot is that he begins to define his world not as
the familiar Conradian sea or wilderness of contingent and unpredictable forces, but as "the balance of colossal forces" and of "perfect
equilibrium." Such appreciation may seem very philosophic, and it
may seem to point to Stein as an oracle of as much beauty and grace as
the prize butterfly possesses, but in the context of Conrad's early sea
fiction Stein's attitudes here are unmistakably suspect and full of irony.
That Stein should present himself as an oracle who relishes the "exact"
and the "accurate" very probably suggests that he prefers a world that
is more predictable than beautiful and thus a world that is hardly Marlovian or Conradian. When Marlow interjects in response to this rhapsody
on the perfection of butterfly wings, "And what of man?" (p. 126),
Stein actually exposes himself by replying that man is not a masterpiece
but a nuisance: "Man is come where he is not wanted, where there is no
place for him. . . . Why should he run about here and there making a
great noise about himself, talking about the stars, disturbing the blades
of grass?" (p. 126). For Stein man is tantamount only to a mistake, to a
disruption of harmony and precision. Much like the lieutenant who because of his rigid devotion to honor refuses to indulge in subtle considerations of other people's problems, Stein here betrays such a strong
dependence upon cosmic predictability that he, too, must become a
questionable commentator upon Jim's affairs—if he does condescend to
address them.

Marlow, however, does not allow the reader to condemn this oracle
so easily. For when Marlow finally relates the tale of Jim's failures, he
notes that Stein then begins to divest himself of his air of pompous phi-
losophizing and to show some genuine interest. Suddenly, in fact, while
considering man's entrapment within romantic dreams of sainthood or
deviltry, Stein's definitive and confident manner turns hesitant and uneasy, as if he is speaking from the heaviness of personal experience. Indeed, when he sadly alludes to "the real trouble—the heart pain—the
world pain" that results from man's failure to keep his eyes closed and

inwardly focused upon himself as a fine fellow, he separates himself from his butterfly world of perfect equilibrium and thus, while returning the case of dead butterflies that he has been examining to its catacomb, reveals a dramatic change. As he passes out of the circle of light from the study lamp and into the "shapeless dusk" of the catacombs, the captain notes that his movement develops

> an odd effect—as if these few steps had carried him out of this concrete and perplexed world. His tall form, as though robbed of its substance, hovered noiselessly over invisible things with stooping and indefinite movements; his voice, heard in that remoteness where he could be glimpsed mysteriously busy with immaterial cares, was no longer incisive, seemed to roll voluminous and grave—mellowed by distance. (P. 130)

Somewhat facetiously one might suggest here that the noiseless hovering, the insubstantiality, and the stooping and indefinite movements point to a renewed vitality in Stein as butterfly. If one considers the butterfly as a traditional image of the spirit, there is even some warrant for such a possibility. But this point requires no such exaggeration. It is enough to recognize that Stein in this shapeless gloom is again feeling the heart pains that accompany every pursuit of a fine dream and that surely have accompanied his own pursuits in Celebes in the past.

In the face of Marlow's need for advice, Stein first defines the basic origin and nature of human suffering—that it derives principally from the disturbing tensions that accompany any disparity between dream and actuality—and then, his body having lost its substance, his voice its incisiveness, he approaches his proud moment in the interview and, perhaps, his proudest since he has fled Celebes. It is now that he shares with the bewildered Marlow a truth that he once knew well but that he has for years avoided in the solitude among butterflies. Now he speaks those lines that have fascinated so many readers of Conrad:

> Very funny this terrible thing is. A man that is born falls into a dream like a man who falls into the sea. If he tries to climb out into the air as inexperienced people endeavour to do, he drowns—*nicht war* [sic]? . . . No! I tell you! The way is to the destructive element submit yourself, and with the exertions of your hands and feet in the water make the deep, deep sea keep you up. (P. 130)

I have no intention of fully explicating these lines one more time. What interests me, more than the lengthy and necessary discussions of terms and equations that Guerard and Warren[7] (among others) have expended on the lines, is the precise nature of the metaphor within the passage. For the purposes of this discussion it is more important to note not how the metaphor "translates" into everyday experience, but how the metaphor qualifies the reader's perception of Stein's character and his philosophy of order. By couching his statement in a metaphor of the sea, Stein shifts ground from the perfect equilibrium of cosmic order to the always dynamic forces of contingency. Such a shift is of staggering importance for a Stein who seems set in his ways.

It is true that even in this statement Stein envisions some balance— the swimmer will neither try to climb out into the air (as does the romantic Jim) nor suicidally resign himself to sinking into the depths (as does the disillusioned Brierly) but will try to balance himself by submitting to the sea and there swimming (as does the Marlow who balances cosmic and immediate perspectives). In effect, however, by suggesting that the swimmer balances himself at the surface of the sea, Stein may be regarding swimming as another of those many situations that illustrate "the balance of colossal forces." Such an interpretation, of course, presents a major problem, for it almost forces the reader to conclude that Stein, even when he transfers his attention to Jim's problems, neither enjoys himself nor counsels others to enjoy a life of risk in the wilderness or at sea. Ultimately, in fact, this interpretation reduces Stein's supposedly proud moment of insubstantial hovering to a middle-of-the-road course of exertion and counsel that merely preserves such dreamers as Jim and Brierly from the dangers at the extremes of rarity of air and density of sea. Such an interpretation helps underscore the fundamental sterility of an old philosopher who has already reduced his own life to the inhabiting of butterfly catacombs, but it also turns this most famous of passages from *Lord Jim* into terrible irony.

It is possible, however, to consider the metaphor in the passage from another angle. Other scholars have carefully avoided giving an ironic reading to this passage, and here, too, the problems that the metaphor of the swimmer creates can be evaded if I return to the larger metaphoric situation of the interview. I have already pointed out that shortly before his major pronouncement Stein becomes a hovering spirit[8] and that this change reveals his sudden readiness to speak wisely not about dead butterflies but about troubled man. By assuming, then, that Marlow (with Conrad's help) is developing a consistent metaphor, and also that Stein will quite naturally comment upon even the most dynamic situation in terms of familiar thought patterns, the reader can discover here some new subleties in Marlow's handling of the interview.

Stein's metaphor of the swimmer is marvelously consistent with his earlier comments on balance, and yet it also reveals a resiliency that the earlier comments do not possess. For it is not necessary to regard the swimmer merely as the precise midpoint, the balance, between the man in the air and the man at the bottom of the sea. Nor is it necessary to conclude that the swimmer is merely exerting himself in a desperate attempt to survive. In this moment of insubstantial hovering Stein unquestionably limits the potential space for man's self-realization; that is, man must seek neither all air nor all water. At the same time, however, he allows man all the space that he needs for his development—the almost limitless and always-changing surfaces of the sea. The implicit metaphor of the surface is crucial here because it exposes, from Stein's viewpoint, the nature of man's exertions to survive: at the surface man confronts not a rigid and perfect equilibrium but a limitless series of risks that upset his expectations of equilibrium and that, as a consequence, prompt in him change and development. For Stein, therefore, the surface of the sea is essentially the initiator of change. When he suggests that the swimmer must submit to the destructive element, he is actually emphasizing the fact that man's life is an inescapable situation requiring submission, but also a situation of untold possibilities, of unexpected opportunities, of tensions and vicissitudes that (at the same time that they require submission) provoke new discoveries and self-realization.

For a moment, then, while he is hovering in shapeless gloom, this philosopher who has reduced his own life by retreating from Celebes does offer a comment about man's dilemma that both Marlow and Conrad can accept. That moment, however, is short-lived because immediately upon completing his comment upon the destructive element, Stein recovers his voice ("his voice leaped up extraordinarily strong") and hastily returns to the bright circle of the lamp. In that light he loses the inspiration and the quiet assurance that have characterized his exalted mutterings. He may wish to continue his remarks, to savor the spectacular insight that he has briefly enjoyed, but when he tries to speak there is no sound. At that point he may suggest, as though his insight has ultimately been beyond verbal articulation, that "there were things . . . that perhaps could never be told" (p. 130), but the reader knows that he is kidding only himself. Indeed, when he finally does repeat his counsel about immersion in the destructive element, the reader fully recognizes that then, much like the stubborn French lieutenant at the end of the other interview, he has rather pathetically reduced his once brilliant insight to mere emphasis upon an exertion that is tantamount only to stoic endurance, not to self-realization: "That was the way. To follow the dream, and again to follow the dream—and so—*ewig*—*usque ad finem* . . ." (p. 131). In the repetition there is no sense of flexibility, no allowing of the dream or its pursuit to be modified amid the vicissitudes of the sea. The dynamic nature of the earlier sea metaphor is missing.

By this point, with Stein's return to his comfortable solitude, the reader has come full circle with the old philosopher. For Marlow, however, the interview is not yet finished. Marlow is the one character in the novel who never entirely ignores the tension between the cosmic and the immediate, between submission and exertion, and thus when he finds himself almost as bewildered before Stein's final counsel as before Jim's dilemma, the reader must be especially careful about responding to Stein's final remarks. Marlow himself has discovered that

> the whisper of [Stein's] conviction seemed to open before me a vast and uncertain expanse, as of a crepuscular horizon on a plain at dawn—or was it, perchance, at the coming of the night? One had not the courage to decide, but it was a charming and deceptive light, throwing the impalpable poesy of its dimness over pitfalls—over graves. (P. 131)

If it can be assumed (and I think it can on the basis of metaphoric evidence) that Marlow does appreciate Stein's earlier insight into the need for both submission and exertion, Marlow's reaction here is very revealing. The captain finds Stein's final counsel of endurance also very attractive, and yet at the same time he notes in himself an uncertainty that the reader dares not overlook. It is probably at this moment that an awareness of the metaphoric patterns in the interview provides the most service. Marlow may appear silent or reserved in his judgments of this Stein who will forever remain his friend, but through his metaphor he has helped pinpoint the weakness or the adulteration that he himself sees in Stein's final counsel. The reader, too, must reject such final counsel of endurance as that of a man who will in the last paragraph of the novel be said to have "aged greatly of late" and who will have shown, consequently, the most profound diminishing of spirit within the whole novel.

Both interviews, then, first with the lieutenant and then with the philosopher, are shrewdly conceived strategies whereby Conrad misleads those readers who ignore the qualifications inherent in Marlow's patterns of metaphor and irony. Many readers may yet regard the lieutenant and Stein as the keys to understanding *Lord Jim*. Here, however, as a result of the preceding exploration of the consistency of Marlow's narrative, it should be clear that Conrad himself probably enjoys an altogether different perception of the two men and their visions. It is true that Stein at least, unlike the lieutenant, does enjoy the grace of a moment's brilliant insight and, further, that this insight (as in Robert Penn Warren's introduction to *Nostromo*) may serve as a marvelous basis for approaching the whole of Conrad's work. Conrad, nevertheless, carefully qualifies the character of Stein too, and eventually one need have no doubt that both Stein and the lieutenant are fools who are afraid to face up to the demands and risks of human existence. Indeed, with their supposed wisdom and insight, both finally serve only as terrible foils for the genius of Marlow's own faculties of discernment and understanding.

# 8

# "Typhoon": Ironic Diminishing of the Pattern

*Lord Jim*, as has been seen in the last two chapters, possesses little immediate relationship to the tradition of navigation that generally informs Conrad's fiction from 1897 to 1902. That fact need not detract from my general thesis, however, for if—as seems likely given Marlow's emphasis upon interviews in the narrative—Conrad is principally interested not in defining man's relationship to the contingent world of the sea or of the jungle but in exploring the possibilities and the limitations of man's relationships with his fellow beings, *Lord Jim* probably still functions as the culmination of all Conrad's theme and artistry in the fiction from *Almayer's Folly* to *Heart of Darkness*. Here, of course, it must be remembered that in *Heart of Darkness*, with the relationship between Marlow and Kurtz, Conrad has already begun to move in the direction of the great theme of relationship between men. Even if Marlow's relationship with Kurtz seems embryonic when juxtaposed to his dealings with Jim and Jewel and with Stein, it is still true that Conrad in this novel is shifting focus from man's relationship with the universe to his relationship with men.[1] Thus, while one may wish to agree with those critics who cite Marlow's rather solitary maturation in the Congo as a justification for considering *Heart of Darkness* Conrad's greatest work from the period, I would point to Marlow's supreme moment of insight while dealing with Jewel as justification for regarding *Lord Jim* as the finer of the two works. To be sure, it may not matter much which of the

121

two works one finally prefers, but at least it is now clear that both on thematic grounds (Marlow's final maturation concerning relationships) and on aesthetic grounds (Marlow's ambiguous patterns of metaphor and irony) *Lord Jim* does serve as the culmination of Conrad's effort before 1900.

With "Typhoon," "Falk: A Reminiscence," and "The End of the Tether," the three principal works that immediately follow *Lord Jim*, Conrad returns to the more rigorous navigational focus of the early sea period. After *Heart of Darkness* and *Lord Jim*, obviously enough, these three tales can hardly enjoy the same philosophic and artistic stature among readers of Conrad's work. One must, nevertheless, guard against reducing these tales to trivial exercises. One critic has suggested that in "Typhoon," the first of the three tales, Conrad's "preoccupations are nearly all on the surface, and [thus that] the devil's share of unconscious creation [is] very slight."[2] Another critic has similarly suggested that this novella "is one of Conrad's simplest important tales, and has none of the ambiguous moral and philosophical overtones with which 'Heart of Darkness' or *Lord Jim* reverberates."[3] This emphasis upon simplicity, however, disregards much of the drama within the tale—notably the tension that develops in the imaginative Jukes as circumstances force him (and the reader) to reappraise the dull Captain MacWhirr's character. Such tension is important, not only because it promotes much of Jukes's change of perspective during the course of the *Nan-Shan*'s voyage, but also because it reveals Conrad's gradual reworking of the navigational metaphor that yet remains the crucial matter of his early fiction. Conrad may with "Typhoon" continue to explore his great theme, the relationship between men, but in this novel he turns the relationship in *Lord Jim* between the perceptive Marlow and the foolish Jim into a fairly humorous irony: the young Jukes, the figure of insight, must depend upon the older MacWhirr, the figure of dull wit, for support during the typhoon. Such a reversal of roles points to a fundamental change in Conrad's use of navigational metaphor. The fact that the maturing Jukes must depend upon a dull MacWhirr essentially limits his opportunity for growth and ultimately defines the terror of modern man's existence within a limited world that has lost most of its glorious, heroic traditions. With "Typhoon" and the two succeeding tales, as a result, one must begin to anticipate the steady diminishing of freedom that is inherent in Conrad's earlier use of the navigational metaphor.

Perhaps the most direct approach to the ironic reworking in "Typhoon" lies in a brief contrast of this short novel with *The Nigger of the*

*"Narcissus."* In terms of plot alone, as shall be explained more fully
later, the similarities between these two novels is very striking: a progression from moral ambivalence to the ravaging of a gale and finally to
the threat of mutiny defines the action of both novels. In "Typhoon,"
of course, the moral ambivalence attaches not to a whole crew but only
to the imaginative Jukes; there, furthermore, the gale becomes the catastrophic typhoon that probably would have destroyed the *Narcissus*; and
there the sense of mutiny colors the coolies', not the crew's, response to
a nightmarish situation. The basic progression is still the same, however, with each novel concluding on the note of disembarking, of having reached port. Naturally, there are also some huge differences
between the two works, and the most important of these is that with
"Typhoon" there is a switch from the world of sails to the world of
steam. In *Heart of Darkness* and *Lord Jim* two steamers have already
appeared—the Congo riverboat and the *Patna*—but in both those novels
the tradition of sailing, with its emphasis upon artistry and self-responsibility, continues to prevail either in the narrating Marlow's consciousness or in the very real fact that he commands a schooner (as in *Lord
Jim*). In "Typhoon" the reader is taken altogether outside the
comfortable world of sails, the world of craft and seamanship, and into
the sphere of machinery, where, according to Conrad, man's trust in the
material separates him from a genuine understanding of the sea and its
nature. The given in this new world is that the officers of the *Nan-Shan*
cannot, at least by virtue of their office aboard the steamer, expect to
learn what their counterparts aboard schooners and barques needed to
know in order to bring their sailing vessels to port after long and arduous
voyages.

Such a given has profound consequences for Conrad's narrative.
Consider, for example, Conrad's development of MacWhirr's character. In contrast to the wonderful Allistoun, who is fully rooted in the
traditions of seamanship, MacWhirr is a grocer's son who somehow
winds up at sea and becomes a success, the nature of such an achievement being highly questionable because it is not rooted in genuine
understanding. Early in the novel the third-person narrator points to the
problem: "having just enough imagination to carry him through each
successive day, and no more, [MacWhirr] was tranquilly sure of himself" (p. 4). The successful MacWhirr may survive each day and ultimately may even seem very confident, but because he possesses so little
imagination, the only world in which he is finally comfortable is the
world of silent routine. Each day he gives his orders and then relaxes

into silence, seemingly comfortable in the presumption that "the more general actualities of the day required no comment" (p. 9). At one point, in fact, having observed Juke's incessant conversation with the third engineer, the captain nearly berates his mate for disturbing the ship's calm with unnecessary chatter: "I can't understand what you find to talk about. . . . Two solid hours. . . . Must be saying the same things over and over again" (pp. 17-18). MacWhirr is dull, and, as Jukes writes a friend in the Western ocean trade, "outside the routine of duty [MacWhirr] doesn't seem to understand more than half of what you tell him" (p. 17). Unquestionably, the captain is trapped within his mental limitations. Such entrapment, however, is only half his problem. The other half is that he, like Jim on the *Patna*, and perhaps like most officers on steamers in Conrad's rubric,

> had never been given a glimpse of immeasurable strength and of immoderate wrath, the wrath that passes exhausted but never appeased—the wrath and fury of the passionate sea. . . . Captain Mac-Whirr had sailed over the surface of the oceans as some men go skimming over the years of existence to sink gently into a placid grave, ignorant of life to the last, without ever having been made to see all it may contain of perfidy, of violence, and of terror. (Pp. 18-19)

Here, of course, MacWhirr's fundamental unsuitability for life in Conrad's seas becomes the real focus of the narrator's concern.

MacWhirr, then, is Conrad's first major representative of the modern seamen who are divorced from the art and craft of their profession. Unlike Allistoun, who instinctively knows what leadership and direction he must provide in the face of a horrendous gale, MacWhirr, having trusted in his steamer to carry him on schedule from port to port, does not understand what principles of navigation he must observe when approaching the typhoon. When he first observes the uncommon fall of the barometer that presages the typhoon, for example, he easily ignores the omen by concluding that there is merely some "dirty weather" in the offing. Eventually, with no change in the barometric conditions, he does experience some dismay and at that point begins to consult a textbook on "storm strategy" for illumination on the problem. As the narrator points out, MacWhirr, in order to achieve his certificate as master some years ago, had "to answer certain simple questions on the subject of circular storms such as hurricanes, cyclones, typhoons" (p. 20). Now, however, having for years skimmed over the surfaces of the sea, he finds those answers entirely meaningless and, therefore, a very poor basis for his present reference to a technical book. As he reads the book and tries to contain in his dull mind the unusual conditions before him, in fact, he becomes the object of the narrator's sarcasm:

> He lost himself amongst advancing semi-circles, left- and right-hand quadrants, the curves of the tracks, the probable bearing of the centre, the shifts of wind and the readings of barometer. He tried to bring all these things into a definite relation to himself, and ended by becoming contemptuously angry with such a lot of words and with so much advice, all head-work and supposition, without a glimmer of certitude. (P. 33)

The sarcasm of the passage clearly deflates any potential view of Mac-Whirr as Conrad's hero of strength.[4]

The reduction in seamanship that defines MacWhirr becomes even more obvious when Jukes barges into the chartroom and suggests a fifty-degree change of course into the waves as a means of moderating the ship's terrific rolling. The captain responds:

> You want me to haul a full-powered steamship four points off her course to make the Chinamen comfortable! Now, I've heard more than enough of mad things done in the world—but this.... Steer four points off.... And what afterwards? Steer four points over the other way, I suppose, to make the course good. What put it into your head that I would start to tack a steamer as if she were a sailing-ship? (Pp. 31–32)

At this point of Jukes's interruption, having already consulted the textbook on storm strategy, the captain continues to fear the dirty weather ahead, but he is not so afraid that he will throw over years of past practice. He is the captain of a crack steamer, not of a sailing ship, and while he knows that, much like Jukes, the "old woman" who wrote the book he has been reading would follow a circuitous route and bring the *Nan-Shan* into Fu-chau from the opposite direction "at the tail of this dirty weather," he is not yet ready to turn his command into the occasion for observing the techniques of sailing. He notes, therefore, as justification for his stubborn determination, that "tacking" the steamer would add three hundred miles to the trip and the expense of "a pretty coal bill," and thus that he "couldn't bring [himself] to do that if every word in [that book] was gospel truth." Here, in the act of rationalizing his decision to proceed ahead as if under normal conditions, MacWhirr finally reveals that fundamental belief in material efficiency at sea that fully exposes the steamer officer's separation from genuine understanding of the vicissitudes of the sea. He may think himself wonderfully strong and capable when he announces to Jukes, "A gale is a gale, Mr. Jukes, . . . and a full-powered steam-ship has got to face it" (p. 34), but to Conrad he is nothing more than a dull-witted fool who, because he does not appreciate man's true relationship to the sea, can never serve as a model of true success in the art of navigation. Such impossibility (and the ironies attendant upon it) becomes most apparent if contrasted, now, with the nature of Jukes's development during the tale.

MacWhirr's separation from the imaginative craft of seamanship tends to introduce to the steamer an atmosphere of verbal absurdity that increasingly tests the young first mate's patience and courage. Early in the voyage to Fu-chau, for example, when the second engineer, irritated by the failure of the sailors to ventilate the engine room, suggests that the young mate shove a barometer "down his gory throat" (p. 24), MacWhirr, overhearing, misinterprets the engineer's metaphor as literal statement and nearly denounces the engineer as a violent and profane man. Then, when Jukes springs to the engineer's defense and informs the captain that the man is a "jolly good second," he, too, becomes vulnerable to the captain's misinterpretation. Jukes defends the second as a victim of circumstance: "It's the heat. . . . The weather's awful. It would make a saint swear. Even up here I feel exactly as if I had my head tied up in a woollen blanket" (p. 25). To Jukes's dismay, the innocuous use of saint and blanket metaphors provokes in MacWhirr much the same misunderstanding as did the original metaphor in the engineer's curse. Such misunderstanding, nevertheless, is only the beginning of the young mate's "education."

Consider another instance of verbal absurdity. Taking heart before the ominous signs of weather ahead, Jukes finishes his recording of the log shortly before the winds of the typhoon arrive and addresses the second mate with a cheery remark concerning the weather. The second, fearful of trouble, especially of exposing his own limitations, at first rebuffs Jukes's friendliness. When he does respond, in fact, it is only in reaction to Jukes's offering of a frank yet rather polite curse, "Oh, go to Jericho!" At that point the second mate suggests, "I've known some real good men get into trouble with their skippers for saying a dam' sight less" (p. 29). Here, with his fundamental fear of curses and conversation, the second mate, too, much in the manner of MacWhirr, destroys all possibility for communication and understanding. In this instance, "completely soured by [the] absurdity" (p. 30) in the second mate's attitudes, Jukes finds himself so thoroughly bewildered that when he subsequently enters MacWhirr's chartroom and suggests a change in the *Nan-Shan*'s course in order to make the passengers more comfortable, he is ripe for the culminating moment in the first stage of his maturation. In response to Juke's request, MacWhirr merely berates the mate for mangling the English language: "Why don't you speak plainly? Couldn't tell what you meant. Never heard a lot of coolies spoken of as passengers before. Passengers, indeed! What's come to you?" (p. 31). After the upsetting exchange with the second mate, Jukes has already lost his footing and has begun "to flounder." By the end of the interview with the captain he hears MacWhirr declare, "If I didn't know you, Jukes, I would think you were in liquor." The point in all these details is not merely that MacWhirr and the second mate are dull. It is also that Jukes has lost his verbal confidence. Such a loss suggests that even before the arrival of the full onslaught of the typhoon Jukes has become involved in a terrible process of self-examination that will finally make of him a true seaman despite his serving on a steamer and under a captain of questionable insight and authority.

When the typhoon does arrive, the *Nan-Shan*'s limited world of dullness and misunderstanding turns into a much larger world of verbal and perceptual discontinuity. Repeatedly, whole conversations between MacWhirr and Jukes break down as the winds nullify the power of their voices and toss their words into the clamor of the raging waves. Indeed, in the forty pages of narrative at the heart of the story there are at least ten reminders of the discontinuity that begins with Jukes's "Watch — put in — wheelhouse shutters — glass — afraid — blow in," a shattered comment to which MacWhirr responds, "This — come — anything — warning — call me" (p. 37). In such a discontinuous world, of course, , Jukes quickly discovers how "the disintegrating power of a great wind . . . isolates one from one's kind" (p. 40), for suddenly — much like the young Marlow of the *Judea* who finds his body "describing a short parabola" in the air, he finds himself absorbed into a huge wave that separates him from MacWhirr. This moment, with all of its overtones of death, is particularly critical for Jukes's growth:

> He fancied himself whirled a great distance through the air. Everything disappeared — even, for a moment, his power of thinking. . . .
> His distress was by no means alleviated by an inclination to disbelieve the reality of this experience. . . . [Nevertheless,] the convic-

tion of not being utterly destroyed returned to him through the sensations of being half-drowned, bestially shaken, and partly choked. (P. 41)

In order to steady himself, Jukes grabs hold of a rail-stanchion, but another huge wave loosens his grip, and again he finds himself "suddenly afloat and borne upwards." The metaphor is clear. Having already endured the distresses of verbal absurdity, Jukes now faces the complete nullification of perception, the loss of all bearing and direction and finally of comprehension itself. He is, by virtue of the metaphor, at the point of death or transformation.

The typhoon as a metaphysical entity is wordless, valueless, traditionless, and directionless, and thus it represents both the antithesis and the nullification of all Jukes's past confidence and easy superiority. Before such an ominous entity an immature Jukes might easily and almost justifiably resign himself to his exhaustion, and yet while rolling around haphazardly in the great volumes of water on the steamer's deck, he gradually becomes conscious of himself repeating in desperation, "My God! My God! My God! My God!" (p. 42) and at the same time experiences "a revolt of misery and despair." At that point this young officer actually rejects capitulation to psychic exhaustion or death and resolves — much like the Marlow in the Congo — to attempt an extrication of himself from such circumstances, no matter how hopeless articulation (physical or verbal) may seem to have become. It is while acting upon this resolution that Jukes manages to "become somehow mixed up with a face, an oilskin coat, somebody's boots" and thus to find his captain. Again the metaphor is very striking and this time also ironic. For if Jukes now begins, by virtue of his new resolution, to mature into an officer (captain) who can himself fulfill the traditions and duties of command even in a typhoon, the narrative also seems to suggest that such maturation is very dependent upon the moral support that only the dull MacWhirr can provide.

Jukes has found that the storm has "weakened his faith in himself" or that, when he desperately tries to identify the person with whom he has become tangled, "his temples [seem] ready to burst." Moreover, even after identifying MacWhirr, he has discovered that he is still ready either to relax into a paralyzing indifference because "there [is] nothing to be done" (p. 45) or to fall prey to "an incredible disposition to somnolence, as though he had been buffeted and worried into drowsiness" (p. 48). Having lost all his confidence, however, he now receives MacWhirr's order to investigate the disorder among the coolies. At first the

mate resists the order. He fears the necessity of encountering the typhoon alone, but he also regards such an assignment as meaningless:
"The absurdity of the demand made upon him revolted Jukes. He was
as unwilling to go as if the moment he had left the deck the ship were
sure to sink" (p. 60). Because he knows only that he wants to survive
the typhoon himself, Jukes cannot understand MacWhirr's stupid desire
to be "fair" to the coolies. And yet, while he determinedly resists the
captain's order by arguing that the coolies will settle their quarrel by
themselves, in this primal conflict of wills the dull but stolid MacWhirr
easily overpowers the uncertain mate, and eventually Jukes realizes that
he has no other alternative but to go. It is at this point, ironically, that
MacWhirr's command becomes the key to the possibility of Jukes's
thorough transformation.

When Jukes reaches the crew in the dark alleyway leading to the
'tween deck of the coolies, he still feels as though he wants to "throw
himself down amongst them and never move any more" (p. 61). Or
when he enters the bunker leading to the coolies' deck and hears their
screaming, he yet again feels his head swim and his resolution waver.
Indeed, after surveying the "regular little hell" of the coolies tumbling
after their money, and after descending into the stokehold and there discovering "a place deep as a well, black as Tophet," a place where fire
becomes "a pool of flaming blood" and where language degenerates
into nothing more than "a stream of curses upon all things on earth,"[5]
he probably approaches the moment of his greatest temptation to capitulate. MacWhirr may earlier have accused him of being in liquor, but in
this pressure of unabated tumult and bewilderment his glance actually
turns "wandering and tipsy" (p. 70). Then, when the climactic wave of
the typhoon thrusts the steamer "over the edge of the world," he even
begins to bawl. At that point, understandably enough, his face turns
"hopelessly blank and gentle, like the face of a blind man" (p. 74)
—as if he were resigning himself to his exhaustion. At that moment,
however, he also hears the captain's confirmation of the command to restore order among the coolies. The captain's determination now makes
the difference.

It is true that after hearing the confirmation Jukes initially staggers
away from the speaking tube "like a defeated man from the field of bat-
tle"; further, that when he darts into the 'tween deck,

> another lot of coolies on the ladder, struggling suicidally to break
> through the battened hatch to a swamped deck, fell off as before, and
> [Jukes] disappeared under them like a man overtaken by a

landslide. . . . In the instant he had been lost to view, all the buttons of his jacket had gone, its back had got split up the collar, his waistcoat had been torn open. (P. 77)

In this landslide Jukes knows the worst of experiences — that of being overwhelmed by the very inferno he is sent to subdue. And yet when the boatswain, worried that the mate may "be trampled *to death*" (emphasis added), urges the crew to rescue him, Jukes emerges from the confusion of the coolies' bodies by himself and yells, "Leave me alone — damn you. I am all right." Suddenly, in the very moment when he seems to have most reason to despair and to capitulate, but in the moment when action becomes absolutely necessary in the primary sense of preserving himself, Jukes recovers the voice of confident articulation. Displaying a readiness that defines him as a matured officer, he now gives his men specific orders and executes the mission with which he has been entrusted. At that point, furthermore, he becomes conscious of having managed the typhoon: "In his mad struggle . . . he had overcome the wind somehow. . . . a silence had fallen upon the ship" (p. 79). With Jukes's recovery of the world of meaning and direction, the first half of the typhoon diminishes to a lull.[6]

At the beginning of the last chapter of this novella the narrator suggests that the *Nan-Shan* has during the typhoon sighted "the coast of the Great Beyond, whence no ship ever returns to give up her crew to the dust of the earth" (p. 91). In addition, he suggests that Jukes, upon leaving the 'tween deck and regaining the bridge, discovers that he "could detect obscure shapes as if his sight had become preternaturally acute" (p. 80). Both details, of course, probably underscore Jukes's realization of the necessity of articulating even in the most untoward of situations. It is not until MacWhirr leaves the bridge and enters the chart room, however, that the true nature of Jukes's maturation becomes clear. For when MacWhirr leaves, the mate again becomes conscious of anxiety — "as if the storm were sure to pounce upon him as soon as he had been left alone with the ship" (p. 83) — and the result of such anxiety is that the reader must remain skeptical about Jukes's supposed growth.[7] If one examines the narrator's skein of ironies, the reason for such skepticism becomes immediately visible.

The fact that Jukes matures while first mate aboard a steamer is by itself an irony of some proportion, given Conrad's basic attitudes toward steam. That irony is rather insignificant, however, when compared to the irony in Jukes's dependence upon the dull MacWhirr. I do not want to argue here that Jukes during this voyage of the *Nan-Shan* becomes another MacWhirr, a captain who, with all his limitations, hardly appears a seaman of the first order, and yet the suggestive detail of Jukes's finding his captain must not be overlooked. In a real sense this short novel is about Jukes's maturation into captaincy or, at least, into responsible officership, and because it is MacWhirr who first supports this mate by catching hold of him "round the waist" and who then provides him with the opportunity for growth via the execution of a command, MacWhirr tends to serve as the model for Jukes's maturation. Certainly when the mate himself perceives the tremendous difficulty of executing MacWhirr's directive and yet proceeds to carry out his mission, his "determination" smacks of MacWhirr's own dogged devotion to routine. In fact, when during the lull near the end of the novel he embraces MacWhirr's counsel about what he — Jukes — must do if the second onslaught of the typhoon sweeps the captain off deck, he seems to offer solid confirmation of the possibility that he has become another Mac-Whirr. MacWhirr has said: "Keep [the *Nan-Shan*] facing it. They may say what they like, but the heaviest seas run with the wind. Facing it — always facing it—that's the way to get through. You are a young sailor. Face it. That's enough for any man. Keep a cool head" (p. 89). After his harrowing experiences and especially after a long series of temptations to capitulate to his exhaustion, Jukes understandably appreciates the importance of such counsel. The terrible irony in this novel, then, is that this imaginative mate, perhaps representative of modern youth, eventually depends upon a dull MacWhirr for support and guidance when MacWhirr understands little of that Conradian world represented in the always-changing sea. To the extent that the mate, upon MacWhirr's return to the deck from the chart room, experiences another "access of confidence, a sensation that came from outside like a warm breath, and made him feel equal to every demand" (p. 89), he must appear as another MacWhirr who now values the ethic of endurance. With his imagination, of course, Jukes may ultimately become much more than MacWhirr, maybe even an officer of the first order, and yet there is in this novel the profound sense that he shall never enjoy the almost unlimited maturation of the perspicacious Marlow. Jukes does not belong to the heroic world of sails, and his maturation, while very real, shall probably remain limited even in the future — at least if compared, say, to the young Marlow's on the *Judea* or in the Congo.

The narrator's ambiguous handling of Jukes's maturation is not the end of his skein of irony. MacWhirr, too, despite his dullness, knows some increase in perspective and thus of self-growth. Throughout the novel he may speak only in platitudes or brevities or he may appear the fool for not having steamed around the typhoon, but when he finally accepts the fact that "according to the books the worst is not over" (p. 81) or when, during the lull, he actually thinks of the comfort of the "passengers" whom he at the beginning of the voyage has largely ignored, he reveals some adjustment of perspective — no matter how slight. Indeed, when he enters his chart room during the lull and consults the barometer and the aneroid glass, he faces a disorder of his personal possessions that finally necessitates a genuine accommodation: "The hurricane had broken in upon the orderly arrangements of his privacy. This had never happened before, and the feeling of dismay reached the very seat of his composure" (p. 85). In such distress, it is true, he does take delight in the fact that a towel is still hanging on the door of his washstand locker. That towel, like the matchbox that he has already found in its appropriate shelf, may even become "the symbol of all these little habits that chain us to the weary round of life" (p. 85) and, therefore, the guarantee that MacWhirr's order of life shall retain much of its effectuality. In general, nevertheless, this captain is now very conscious of his new appreciation of the validity and the necessity of storm strategy. When he returns to deck, he may at first rather typically suggest to Jukes, "She [the *Nan-Shan*] may come out of it yet" (p. 86), but at the same time he also acknowledges to Jukes his new respect for strategy: "If we only can steam her round in time to meet it . . . " (p. 87). Unquestionably, he has enjoyed some seasoning of vision, and given the narrator's thorough presentation of his dullness earlier in the tale, that seasoning must strike the reader as terribly ironic. It is as if MacWhirr has learned something — despite himself.

There is a further irony in the portrayal of MacWhirr. After hearing Jukes's warnings about the mutinous intentions of the coolies (who believe that they have been robbed), the captain by himself rather cleverly manages to divide up the money among all the coolies. Through an interpreter he reasons with them that he shall never be able to establish the rightful amount due to each coolie and, further, that unless he himself divides the money up, some official onshore will pocket the money. The coolies acknowledge the validity of the argument, and thus, whereas the imaginative and seemingly matured Jukes is afraid to permit the coolies access from the 'tween deck, MacWhirr hardly hesitates. The irony is inescapable. Jukes may rush to get the rifles in order to squelch an impending mutiny, but MacWhirr proves the sureness of his insight when he carries off the proceedings with nary an injury. Much like Allistoun, who squelches a mutiny among the crew of the *Narcissus*, he easily manages to contain the imminent threat of the coolies. MacWhirr, however, is a dull-witted fool, not a wise Allistoun, and if by the end of the narrative he has become a character of courage and even of some insight who does manage to right the several messes that he has indirectly caused by directing the *Nan-Shan* into the heart of the typhoon, that success must strike the reader as principally ironic.

There is one final, perhaps supreme, irony in the tale. Both Jukes and MacWhirr enjoy a transformation, or at least an adjustment, of perspective, but Solomon Rout, the chief engineer, does not.[8] Such a fact, of course, may seem appropriate if one recalls that the chief engineer is thoroughly identified with the material, or the machinery, that Conrad believes has separated man from the craft of the sea. And yet, unlike Jukes, who merely has a friend in the Western Ocean, or unlike Mac-Whirr, who merely enjoys a pedestrian marriage, or unlike the second mate, who loses his nerve during the typhoon and thus severs (much in the fashion of Donkin at the end of *The Nigger of the "Narcissus"*) all connection with the *Nan-Shan*, Solomon Rout enjoys a wonderfully animated and strong relationship with his wife — who actually turns him into a prophet (akin to the Old Testament king) by parading him among her acquaintances with the prefatory warning, "Solomon says!" By virture of this parading as well as on the strength of those other names (Old Sol or Father Rout) that identify him with religious vision, Rout becomes the wise man aboard the *Nan-Shan* who, unlike the other men, fully understands himself and his desires. In a letter to his wife, for example, he reveals why he likes his berth aboard the *Nan-Shan*: "For my part, . . . give me the dullest ass [MacWhirr] for a skipper before a rogue. There is a way to take a fool; but a rogue is smart and slippery" (p. 16). Rout is shrewd, and yet because he does not expect much in the line of cleverness from MacWhirr, he leaves himself vulnerable to genuine surprise when the captain actually succeeds in his dealings with the coolies. He is so stunned by that success, in fact, that for the first time he fails to communicate to his wife what has happened during the latest trip of the *Nan-Shan*. He is afraid that she will not be able to understand the wonder of MacWhirr's achievement; it is a fear to which she responds with some passion: "How provoking! He doesn't say what it is. Says I couldn't understand how much there was in it. Fancy! What could it be so very clever? What a wretched man not to tell us!" (p. 96). The sagacious Rout, however, by the very fact of being nonplussed, underscores the genius of MacWhirr's handling of the coolies. He may not make the nuances in MacWhirr's feat fully evident to his wife, but he does (with the narrator's help) direct the reader toward the essential ambiguity in MacWhirr's characterization. As the figure of insight who provides such direction, he—the engineer in steam—probably becomes the tale's most delicious irony.

# 9

# "Falk": The Last Maturation

While one must be very skeptical of the use of biographical evidence as the sole basis for any conclusions concerning a story by an author so frequently ironic as Conrad, it is interesting to note that the experience of the narrator in "Falk: A Reminiscence," like that of the narrator in *The Shadow-Line*, is based upon Conrad's own distressing assumption of a first command, the *Otago*, in Bangkok late in January 1888. During the six months preceding the assignment to the *Otago*, from July to December 1887, Conrad had been languishing first in a hospital in Singapore, where he recovered from an injury from a falling spar (the injury that later becomes Lord Jim's), and then as first mate on the *Vidar*, a steamer whose monotonous course becomes the basis for Whalley's *Sofala* trip in "The End of the Tether."[1] One can imagine, therefore, that for the Conrad who has by then become thoroughly committed to the craft and the traditions of sails and yet who during those six months suffered a terrible reduction to the monotony and the immobility of life in the hospital and on the steamer, the appointment to the command of a schooner must have been very exhilarating. When he assumed his new office, however, he immediately discovered that more trouble was in the offing. First he learned that his men were sick after a long delay in port and that his mate, Mr. Born, even required hospitalization. Then he found that he had to endure an excessively long passage to Singapore eight hundred miles away, during which he made the shocking discovery that the previous captain had sold most of the quinine needed for his sick men. Altogether, Conrad's first few weeks on the *Otago* seem al-

135

most catastrophic, and while he did reach Singapore and thereafter began to love his new ship, he probably never forgot how difficult his rise to the supreme joys of seamanship, those of the commander, had proven to be. One should not be surprised, consequently, that the major thrust of "Falk" centers upon how the young captain manages to overcome the difficulties surrounding his assumption of a first command.[2]

In connection with the biographical basis for the story, it might also be noted how "Falk" fits into the context of Conrad's early fiction. With "Youth" and *Heart of Darkness* and even with *Lord Jim*, Conrad employs a first-person narrator who has in the past experienced several genuine maturations. In "Youth" this maturation is rooted in a new understanding of seamanship; in *Heart of Darkness,* in a profound reappraisal of what it means to navigate a world without values or sanctions; and in *Lord Jim*, in an increased understanding of the fundamental necessity, yet the hopelessness, of human relationships. Always, as Marlow matures during the experiences that he later recounts in these three tales, there is the sense of an understanding that is continually enlarging. By the time Conrad writes "Typhoon" and "Falk," however, this process of maturation seems to diminish considerably. One reason for the diminishing is, perhaps, Conrad's relaxation from the tensions of ambiguity that increasingly strain Marlow's first-person narration until *Heart of Darkness* and *Lord Jim* become, for most readers, very confusing and hazy literary works. With the first-person narration of "Falk," Conrad avoids radical experimentation with such a complicated narrator.[3] Instead of continuing to explore the narrative possibilities in an ambiguous Marlow who has already gone through so much, he now merely contents himself with the thematic ironies inherent in the maturations that occur in the world of steam. In a sense, of course, Conrad's retreat from Marlow probably reflects his recognition that, given the fact that the world of navigation has turned to steam, a further enlarging of Marlow's perspective is impossible.

If one remembers, nevertheless, how in "Youth" and in *Heart of Darkness* Marlow's development is closely related to his assumption of a new command, and then how in *Lord Jim* his development is related only to his befriending of Jim the outcast, one can begin to recognize another problem that faced Conrad when he wrote "Falk." In "Falk" Conrad presents a captain who becomes, virtually at the same time that he is rising to the challenges of his first command, the befriender of Falk the outcast. The result is that Conrad finds himself working two different Marlovian angles at once. To be sure, these angles may not be mutually exclusive. After all, in *Heart of Darkness* Marlow himself is at the beginning the new and inexperienced captain of a Congo steamboat and at the end the friend of Kurtz who is the outcast among pilgrims. And yet, despite the similarities between *Heart of Darkness* and "Falk," there is one fundamental difference between the two tales: in the earlier tale Marlow's maturation in the Congo is largely complete before he reaches Kurtz and forever becomes his ally, while in "Falk" the captain becomes heavily involved in a conflict with Falk before he has demonstrated his ability to navigate Conrad's world of moral nothingness.[4] That difference is crucial, and it suggests that Conrad with this tale, much as he had already done in "Typhoon," is reworking his old paradigm of self-realization for new and striking thematic effects. Again, consequently, the reader must be prepared for the advent of more irony.

In the preceding chapter I established the nature of the new irony that characterizes Conrad's handling of the relationship between Jukes and MacWhirr. In "Falk," too, Conrad continues to explore man's relationships, here between a young captain and Hermann, then between the captain and Falk, and again the exploration is essentially focused upon the ironies of modern man's living within a world that has suffered a tremendous transformation (or, according to Conrad, a diminishing). For just as Jukes's growth ironically depends upon the dull MacWhirr's support, so the young captain's growth in "Falk" will depend upon his bewildering relationship with the skipper of a tugboat who is little more than an outcast. At the same time, nevertheless, because this captain, unlike Jukes, enjoys a maturation that is almost the equivalent of Marlow's in the Congo, it will quickly become evident that Conrad in "Falk" is actually working against himself — at once both diminishing his paradigm of maturation through irony yet investing that same paradigm with another major maturation. Such a conflict of interest, if its presence can be established, shall go a long way toward explaining the seemingly unsatisfactory conclusion of the tale and, therefore, the uncertainty of most critical reactions to the tale's stature as a whole.

The fact that must control the reader's initial response to "Falk" is that almost as soon as the young captain (he is "not yet thirty") takes command of the barque stranded in an eastern port after her previous captain's death, he becomes the inheritor of a mess of unpaid bills, of papers intimating some bribery, and of a host of doggerel verses that portend little promise of success to his new undertaking and that, especially if coupled with the old first mate's attitude of resistance and the second mate's absolute stupidity, actually isolate the captain from significant human intercourse. This isolation aboard ship is only the beginning of the trouble, however, for as his barque lingers in the heat of the eastern port his crew members succumb, one by one, to the plague. Already at that point, of course, even though he has only recently gained the command, this captain can hardly avoid becoming fully aware of the virtual meaninglessness of his new office. As he some years later narrates: "Altogether I was not getting on. I would discover at odd times (generally about midnight) that I was totally inexperienced, greatly ignorant of business, and hopelessly unfit for any sort of command" (p. 153). At first such an extreme loss of confidence may seem only to equate this captain with the rest of Conrad's early heroes. The Marlow who enters the Congo, for example, endures a similar loss of vocation when he arrives at the Central Station and there discovers that his steamer is lying at the bottom of the river. This young captain, nevertheless, particularly when his temporary steward steals his last thirty-two golden sovereigns, experiences the depression of feeling "as poor and naked as a fakir" (p. 156). Marlow at the Central Station at least continues to enjoy the financial support of the company in Brussels, but this captain loses virtually everything, confidence and money, upon his assumption of a command. His circumstances, therefore, by gradually slipping further and further beyond his control, may constitute the worst situation before any of Conrad's early heroes.

Initially, it is true, the young captain does seek relief from his powerlessness in the company of Hermann on the *Diana*. Daniel Schwarz has even suggested that such a search reflects in the captain a desire for "the 'civilized,' rational values" of the *Diana*[5] and thus a pursuit of mature control over his untoward situation. Perhaps he is right, but I suspect that the issue is not as clear-cut as that. Throughout the story the inexperienced captain does pride himself on a rational approach to the circumstances of his life. Even later, when he becomes thoroughly upset with Falk's mistreatment of him, he still functions as rationally as possible, with every intention of managing the circumstances without losing his moral pride. In this early reliance upon Hermann, however, he betrays a rather significant loss of moral insight. He ignores, for example, his more lucid moments when Hermann's heavy and good-natured appearance strikes him not as that of a seaman, but as that of "a well-to-do farmer" or of a "small shopkeeper" (pp. 147–48). Or instead of fully appraising the effects upon himself of his reliance upon Hermann, he merely takes delight in the fact that aboard the *Diana* he feels relieved of the pressures upon his own ship. Years later, while narrating, he may regard the name of the *Diana* as "an impertinence towards the memory of the most charming of goddesses" (p. 149), but at the time of his distress he regards the ship not as an object of ridicule but as "a most innocent old ship" that "seemed to know nothing of the wicked sea" and to which "no whisper of the world's iniquities had ever penetrated" (p. 156). For him the dazzling green and white *Diana* then becomes the immaculate world of "meticulous neatness . . . arduously explored — with toothbrushes" (p. 157) or a world of "arcadian felicity" (p. 158) that sharply contrasts with his own. She may seem a world of civilized values, and thus worthy of his attention, but in the face of the rash of troubles aboard his own ship the captain's attraction to the *Diana* essentially argues a moral escapism that hardly promises successful adjustment to the rigors of his new office.

With the intrusion of Falk into the *Diana*'s world of innocence, of course, the young captain gradually begins to separate himself from the moral relaxation and self-delusion that prevent his rise to capable leadership. Already in the initial encounters with Falk, the confused captain generally finds himself at a loss to explain Falk's silence and uncommon behavior. He notes, for example, that Falk will sometimes say "a few low words . . . , half a dozen at most" (p. 161) as a parting gesture to Hermann's wife and niece, but he finds that such words are hardly enough to redeem the rest of the gruff man's conduct, especially the mutters and stares that characterize the majority of each visit. Then, too, he notes that Falk repeatedly "draw[s] the palms of both his hands down his face, giving at the same time a slight, almost imperceptible, shudder" (p. 163). At best, the captain finds such a habit enigmatic, and although he also suspects a tinge of disgust in the shudder, in the context of the deafening silence he at first appreciates only how the habit further isolates Falk from the people about him. Schwarz in this connection has suggested that such conduct makes Falk the representative in the story of "primitive, instinctive values.'"[6] He may be right, but here one must remember that Falk appears as much a part of the civilized world as any of the other characters. His principal influence upon the captain, in fact, occurs not only in a social context and among civilized people but long before the disclosure of his cannibalism, and thus he must essentially represent, no matter how bewildering or enigmatic his conduct might seem, another force of civilization with which the captain must contend. Indeed, in the captain's eyes, as shall be seen shortly, Falk later (following the disclosure of his cannibalism) becomes a thoroughly remarkable exhibit of civilized stature.

It is the enigma of Falk's conduct, nevertheless, that provides the captain with his opportunity for genuine self-realization. For when Falk out of jealousy ignores his earlier arrangements with the young captain and tows, instead, the *Diana* and Hermann's niece downriver out of the captain's reach, the captain finally awakens from his moral relaxation and perceives "all the unreason, all the fatuous unreason, of our complacency" in a world beyond prediction. It is a typical awakening in Conrad's early sea fiction, an awakening to the harshness of life's contingencies, and it reduces an already depressed captain to the ravaging of distraught self-consciousness: "How insignificant and contemptible I must appear, for the fellow to dare to treat me like this—I reflected suddenly, writhing in silent agony" (p. 177). Outside Siegers's office, where he initially seeks redress against Falk's misdealing, his new consciousness of himself as "a foolish figure" even brings him to the brink of despair: "I perceived myself involved in hopeless and humiliating absurdities that were leading me to something very like a disaster. 'Let us be calm,' I muttered to myself, and ran into the shade of a leprous wall. . . . For a moment I felt myself about to go out of my mind with worry and desperation" (p. 188). Such despair, however, does not prevent the captain from facing up to the realities of his situation. He knows that he needs Falk's assistance to get downriver and out to sea away from the heat. He may consider other alternatives to Falk's tugging, such as sailing or dragging anchor downriver, but he recognizes that his knowledge of such operations and of the river itself is only theoretical. Indeed, he does not even know what idiosyncrasies of movement his new ship possesses. Ultimately, therefore, he acknowledges to himself that the dangers before him, even if he should gain the help of a former pilot named Johnson, now dissipated, are extreme.

Unlike other of Conrad's early heroes, who have not become involved in situations in which all circumstances appear beyond their control, this captain seems to possess no chance at all for resolving his difficulties. The captain's situation is terrible, and yet at the very moment when he seems on the verge of giving up, when he takes his head between his hands in despair over the "obviousness of [both his] innocence" (p. 194) and his ineffectuality, or when he seems ready to surrender to his fate by foolishly "ascrib[ing] an extraordinary potency to agents in themselves powerless" (p. 195) — it is then, ironically, that he discovers in himself a genius for handling his bewildering situation. For upon the arrival of Falk himself in Schomberg's coffee room, this young captain suddenly, without thinking, seizes the opportunity and determinedly confronts the taciturn tugboat skipper with the necessity of having a talk. The rest of Schomberg's customers, of course, expect a "stag fight" between the two men, who are supposedly the principals in a contest for the affections of Hermann's niece. Instead, however, the young captain easily manages to lead a "suddenly tractable" Falk quietly into the fresh air of the open verandah and there initiate a private discussion. The other customers continue to stare expectantly at the principals through the window, and Schomberg himself becomes more and more anxious over the breaking of one of the panes, but by that point the young captain has already discovered in himself a remarkable presence of mind. Coolly asking for a pack of cards, a couple of lights, and two long drinks, he manages — by virtue of such a request — not only to soothe Schomberg's fear for his property, but also to isolate the two men from the other customers' interference. The upshot is that he gains for himself his first real opportunity for unraveling all those difficulties that, only moments before, had seemed beyond his control.

This situation, in fact, if one remembers the highly ritualized games of survival enacted between Falk and the carpenter of the *Borgmester Dahl* and then between Falk and the other survivors, may be another instance of the importance of game strategy.[7] In this situation of strained circumstances, the young captain, if only intuitively, quickly recognizes the necessity of providing some genuine defense for himself and Falk. Much as Falk (on the mutinous *Borgmester Dahl*) finally had to assert some control over the game of cannibalism by gaining possession of all the matches and the revolvers, so here the captain realizes that as long as he and Falk seem to be playing cards (Falk in fact knows no card games), he shall defend his discussion with Falk from outside interference. At the same time, of course, he hopes to turn the discussion into a resolution of the conflict that has arisen between the two men. In these terms, it should be clear, the game as a defense against outside interference and as a shrewd device for resolution becomes a particularly complicated imaginative act.

Perhaps because in the card game he is no longer languishing in the false innocence of Hermann's *Diana*, the captain here makes the startling, yet very mature, discovery of how much the enigmatic Falk is like himself—with a desire both for respectability and for companionship that nearly overshadows in intensity his own desire to become an effective and respected captain. To be sure, the young officer may seem to regard Falk as some representative of natural forces or as a man whose only concern seems to be "self-preservation," but finally, in the context of his new discovery of Falk's essential being, he notes that Falk's silence and egoism function primarily as masks for deeper feelings. For him, in fact, Falk's masks now serve as the devices by which Falk perpetuates his life following the psychic upheaval of cannibalism, and as conscious masks they introduce the young captain to even further imaginative understanding. While playing at cards, and while focusing upon Falk's demeanor, this captain has actually realized that masks are the means by which every man, even a man as strong as Falk, seeks to satisfy his inner desires, and thus that masks constitute the range of freedom (or the range of alternatives) with which man pursues his satisfactions. In Falk's case, for example, the desire for respectability leads to the adoption of various masks of superiority. Ironically, however, when the desire for affection results in the pursuit of Hermann's niece, such masks, say, of pride and silence, reduce Falk to a rather strange and sometimes painfully humorous courtship. For a long time the young captain himself may not conceive what Falk's "game" is; he is very shocked, for instance, to discover that he is a supposed rival to this proud tugboat skipper for the affections of Hermann's niece. While gaming on the verandah, therefore, having finally understood the nature and the necessity of Falk's masks, the captain achieves a profound growth of insight and thus is ready to free himself of the paralysis that has characterized his inaction during the past several weeks. He himself now prepares for "mask" existence.

The discovery of the necessities and the possibilities inherent in mask existence functions as the climax of the young captain's self-realization. Indeed, in view of his success with the card game, this captain now proposes yet another game in order to put the lie forever to Falk's anxiety concerning his—the captain's—involvement with the niece: he will speak to Hermann on Falk's behalf and will thus become, himself, a participant in the game of Falk's courtship. With this proposal the young captain freely and consciously adopts for himself a new mask and thus, for the first time since becoming captain, discovers a mature confidence in himself and his undertakings: "I felt I held the winning cards" (p. 203). The adoption of such a role, of course, considerably alters his relations with the proud and distant Falk. Because the change is so dramatic, in fact, one may hereafter fully expect him to deal with Falk in as "perfectly straightforward" a manner as Falk has dealt with him. If he has earlier feared Falk, now he badgers the tugboat skipper with a somewhat flippant accusation of bribing Johnson and even with the hazardous reminder of the Vanlo affair. The young captain spares no tricks as he reminds Falk of his past conduct. He knows that the success of his own rise to captaincy depends upon his handling of the present game, but now, in the first moments of genuine relief, he takes thorough delight in "handling" Falk himself. Because he believes that Falk possesses "the hard, straight masculinity that would conceivably kill but would not condescend to cheat" (p. 210), he has every reason to believe that Falk, heretofore his opponent, will accept his straightforward commentary without seeking revenge. He is right. The captain, with his new level of confidence and insight, is able to turn the tables and to enjoy Falk at Falk's own expense.

The rest of "Falk," although it has received the most attention in the scholarly criticism, is merely attendant upon the moment when the young captain becomes Falk's diplomat. As Falk's ambassador, the captain adopts a new mask and thus identifies himself as the inhabitant of a new world — a world not merely of primitive and instinctive values, as Schwarz suggests, but of that metaphysical emptiness in which it becomes each man's responsibility to create from his own heart the games and the strategies of his action. The emphasis here is upon creation, especially upon the creation of games that are adequate reflections of man's desire, and in the context of such positive emphasis Conrad's readers themselves should probably applaud the captain's glad assumption of "the character of an ambassador." The captain may himself find the assumption of such a role as "all too extravagantly nonsensical," but because he also knows that the role is crucial for any further alleviation of past misunderstandings and thus to his successful transition into the role of captain, he with little hesitation decides to play the role seriously: "I conceived that it would be best to compose for myself a grave demeanour" (p. 210). The ultimate proof of his ability to adopt a new mask and to inhabit this new level of experience, nevertheless, does not appear until he actually confronts Hermann with Falk's will and intention.

In the face of Hermann's narrow-minded outbreak against Falk's supposed cupidity and conceit (p. 211), or his virtuous disregard of the importance of passion (p. 214), or his excessive outrage against Falk's disclosure of past cannibalism (gasping, he manages only to shriek out the one word, "Beast"), the young captain in his new mission seems to enjoy little chance of success. And yet, recognizing what he himself has just learned about the masks of experience, he very shrewdly does not allow himself to be daunted. When Hermann finally begins to calm down, the captain gradually begins to temporize the moral outrage that the portly German — now a fat seal in his eyes — feels: "[The story of Falk's cannibalism] is true just as much as you are able to make it; and exactly in the way you like to make it. For my part, when I hear you clamouring about it, I don't believe it is true at all" (p. 233). Or a bit later: "In all these tales . . . there is always a good deal of exaggeration" (p. 237). The captain here tries to pass on a truth concerning the subjectivity inherent in all vision and action, which he himself has only recently acquired during his dealings with Falk, but the stolid Hermann is not as good a learner. Indeed, if he, with his shopkeeper's mentality, is ever to get over his present moral squeamishness concerning Falk's past, it will not be because he is levitating toward a new level of insight but only because he can rationalize himself into an acceptable business transaction. When he finally hands the girl over to Falk, he suspends his squeamishness not because he suddenly sees — as does the young captain — the remarkable nature of Falk's postcannibal achievements, but because he intends to save the girl's passage money home. Such rationalizing away of moral squeamishness, understandably enough, strikes the captain as absolutely vulgar, and at that point he has no doubt at all which of his two friends is the superior being. Appropriately, it is in reference to Falk (whose name means "falcon" or, ironically, "bird of prey") and not to Hermann (whose name means, ironically, "master man") that the captain now exclaims when the ecstatic Falk picks him up, "What a man!" (p. 220).

Finally, however, if Falk is a man of such depth and insight, why does the narrator insist near the end that he is "dominated . . . by the

singleness of one instinct'' (p. 223), the instinct to live? Does the concentration of energy into one instinct, perhaps as a simplification of
existence, mean that he is less of a man? Or more basic, the primitive
and instinctive man? It seems to me that there is an answer, a very provocative answer in a Laurentian sense, in an organic metaphor that the
narrator includes in his discussion of Falk's singleness of instinct:

> He wanted that girl, and the utmost that can be said for him was that
> he wanted that particular girl alone. I think I saw then the obscure
> beginning, the seed germinating in the soil of an unconscious need,
> the first shoot of that tree bearing now for a mature mankind the
> flower and the fruit, the finite gradation in shades and in flavour of
> our discriminating love. He was a child. He was as frank as a child,
> too. He was hungry for the girl, terribly hungry, as he had been terribly
> hungry for food. (P. 224)

It is easy to conclude in relation to this passage that the narrator is demeaning Falk's passion as something of a child or even of a primitive
''cannibal,'' but such a conclusion sweeps wide of the mark. The
narrator here, with his emphasis upon the ''seed germinating in the soil
of an unconscious need,'' is actually defining as well as he can both the
origin and the sanctions behind the games and masks of conduct in the
mature man's existence. He is suggesting that Falk is wisely shaping the
masks of his life in response to those needs that are instinctively human
and, furthermore, that if one sees in him ''the foundation of all the emotions,'' so one must see that foundation in any man who makes of his
unconscious an arbiter of his fate. Here, therefore, the narrator (and
presumably Conrad) probably comes very close to Lawrence's position
on the relationship of the unconscious to creativity. Such a position, of
course, is a radical departure from, almost the antithesis of, Conrad's
earlier reliance upon the tradition of seamanship as the fount of creativity, and thus this very passage may signal the end of Conrad's use of
navigational metaphor as the ''solution'' to the blackness of human
existence — at least during the period of sea fiction from 1897 to 1902.
Certainly Whalley, Massy, and Sterne, the three principals in Conrad's
next novel, know little, if any, genuine integration of the conscious and
the unconscious, and on that basis all three of them become the damned
characters who entirely exhaust Conrad's previously fertile metaphor of
navigation.

If the reader can accept the terms of the organic metaphor in this passage, the roles of Falk and the young captain in the novel become both

enviable and ironic. For just as the young but matured Marlow appreciates Kurtz's status upon the latter's terrible yet superb awakening at the Congo's Inner Station, so now the young captain fully appreciates Falk, whose ironic vocation as a tugboat skipper tends to make of him another Solomon Rout, as the man with the real core — the man who possesses a vision both of inner desire and of personal responsibility. It is because of this very high regard for Falk, in fact, that the captain gladly continues his services on behalf of Falk. When Hermann at the very end continues to waver between his indignation at Falk and his greed for the girl's passage money, the young captain emphatically assures him on his "own personal knowledge that Falk possessed in himself all the qualities to make his niece's future prosperous" (p. 238). The captain knows that Falk possesses the knowledge of the unconscious that will make him and his wife prosperous and happy. After all, the marriage having already been arranged, both lovers now "come together as if attracted, drawn and guided to each other by a mysterious influence. They were a complete couple" (p. 239). In them the role of the unconscious is obviously very strong. The captain, too, now knows, much like Marlow after the experience in the Congo, how difficult it is "for our minds, remembering so much, instructed so much, informed of so much, to get in touch with the real actuality at our elbow" (p. 226), and thus in addition to appreciating the significance of Falk's present joy, he delights in his own recently developed reliance upon the unconscious. After Falk's heavy influence, this bumbling and seemingly ineffectual captain shall finally look forward—confidently—to directing freely and responsibly his own fate. In these terms he becomes — with Marlow — the man at the heart of Conrad's early vision of freedom and authenticity, and thus despite the structural inadequacy that a number of critics may have found in the narrative, and despite its continued ironic diminishing of man's dependence upon the world of steam, "Falk: A Reminiscence" becomes a much better story, even as a reworking of *Heart of Darkness*, than has to this point been acknowledged.

# 10

## "The End of the Tether": Teleological Diminishing in Conrad's Early Metaphor of Navigation

Near the middle of Conrad's "The End of the Tether" appears a rather striking passage of navigation that critics have to this point ignored. The passage is part of a lengthy sequence of reverie that eventually leads to Sterne's discovery of Captain Whalley's well-guarded secret, but its chief importance lies in the fact that it directs the reader to the crucial metaphor informing the whole tale. That metaphor is, as might be expected, the metaphor of navigation.

In the passage the *Sofala*, after steaming out of Pangu Bay, is entering a "broad lane of water" (p. 241) that stretches for a distance of a hundred miles and that is bounded by perilous reefs and erratic fragments of land. On the whole, the perimeter of the lane may seem to constitute little more than "a foul ground of rocks and shoals," but even in clear and quiet days, too, when the steamer and the reefs are "crushed by the overwhelming power of the light" and the sea lane sometimes "gives no sign of the dangers lurking on both sides of her path" (p. 245), the lane remains an extremely dangerous threat to any hesitant navigation. In the face of such danger, of course, passage by day would seem to be mandatory navigational procedure, and yet, as the narrator is quick to point out, the *Sofala* often makes her way through the lane under cover of night. Since the lane is broad, the trick for the pilot is essentially "to hit upon the entrance correctly in the dark."

Thereafter he must merely follow the compass and trust in his ability to navigate. In such procedure, nevertheless, particularly if the reefs represent the real danger inherent in Conrad's seemingly inescapable wilderness of contingencies, exists abundant opportunity for absolute disaster. Several trips earlier, upon realizing the navigational necessities of maneuvering into this lane, Sterne, the chief mate, has found himself comparing Whalley and his Serang to "an old whale attended by a little pilot-fish" (p. 249). He has long suspected that the active Serang performs most of the maneuvering for the *Sofala*, almost as if he alone were the pilot of the steamer, and upon that trip the mate approaches the full significance of the Serang's role as pilot:

> A pilot sees better than a stranger, because his local knowledge, like a sharper vision, completes the shapes of things hurriedly glimpsed; penetrates the veils of mist spread over the land by the storms of the sea; defines with certitude the outlines of a coast lying under the pall of fog, the forms of landmarks half buried in a starless night as in a shallow grave. (P. 250)

The upshot of this series of associations, generally united by virtue of their exploration of the superior quality of a pilot's perception, is that Sterne begins to suspect his captain of failing eyesight.

When it is remembered, however, that at the end of the novel it is against the reefs of this very sea lane that the *Sofala* disintegrates, Sterne's appreciation, here, of the Serang's superior vision achieves a rather ironic significance: the Serang may successfully direct the *Sofala* into the lane, but his superior vision ultimately proves inadequate. At the same time, if one considers the implications that the passage develops concerning Captain Whalley's blindness, the passage gains another, even more suggestive significance: the blind Whalley, although he may earlier have appeared to Sterne to be rooted in the best tradition of Western seamanship, has become the "stranger" to that tradition because he is no longer an adequate pilot for navigating Conrad's universe of the sea. Such a significance may not be surprising, for given the fact that the last two chapters have already shown how Conrad in "Typhoon" and "Falk" ironically approaches the difficulties of navigating a world in which Western man has become a stranger to a firm tradition of moral and social values, "The End of the Tether" must appear, if only by virtue of its title, as a likely work in which Conrad shall terminate his present interest in navigational metaphor. The fact that the *Sofala* disintegrates at the end of the story, a fact that argues both the failure of the Serang's vision and the compromising of Whalley's career, is proof enough at the outset of this discussion that such a termination does take place.

That Conrad should involve himself in such a task is surely rooted in the fact that he completely exhausted himself in this particularly fertile period of writing from 1897 to 1902. My discussion in a previous chapter has already suggested how Conrad's initial attraction to the possibilities within the metaphor of navigation probably reflects a thorough reaction to his own distress upon the unsatisfactory completion of his first two novels. In both these novels, largely because he is exploring what most critics now accept as a common theme in the novel at the turn of the century, the paralysis of the will, Conrad devotes himself to a rather straightforward and thus limited third-person narrative account of the very personal turmoil that Almayer and Willems endure as white men in an unfriendly universe. Of course, it is probably not so much Conrad's reliance upon the theme and the technique of the late Victorian novelists as it is his own lack of an adequate metaphor that culminates in the — at best — unsatisfying content and style of the two novels. Indeed, the fact that *Almayer's Folly* ends on the note of marriage between Nina and Dain and then with the rejoicing over the birth of their son by itself indicates that Conrad in his first novel already felt it necessary to provide an alternative fate (and its appropriate metaphor) to that of the demoralized Almayer. The metaphor of Nina's pregnancy, however, because it does not fully dramatize the change in her attitudes, is ultimately an inadequate metaphor for her supposedly superior stance. Without a full depiction of the psychological, even philosophical, adjustments she has made, the reader cannot be convinced that her life will turn out appreciably better than her father's. The metaphor fails in the second novel anyway.

What attracts Conrad to the series of tales beginning with *The Nigger of the "Narcissus"* is the teleological possibilities inherent in the metaphor of navigation. Whether one considers the narrator in *The Nigger* (and maybe the narrator of "Karain"), or the young Marlow in "Youth" and *Heart of Darkness*, the older Marlow in *Lord Jim*, Jukes in "Typhoon," or the young captain in "Falk," the one current of metaphoric value that unites all these characters in vision is their rise to the status of navigator. For Conrad, it is now clear, such a rise is testimony not merely to the fact that these seamen have gained the stature of commanders in their profession but that they have achieved a superiority of insight into the nature of their experience, whether past or present. It is true that the younger Marlow's insight in the Congo, or the elder Marlow's into Jim's dilemma in Patusan, is of more weight than, say, Jukes's in "Typhoon," but generally in this period the achievement of mere stature as captain is evidence of the fact that all of these characters have become the privileged, that is, the characters who by superseding the demoralization of an Almayer or a Willems, or of a Kurtz or a Brierly, have actually managed to develop for themselves an alternative fate. To the extent that all these characters have become the privileged, furthermore, they serve as the exhibits of Conrad's consistent reliance throughout the period from 1897 to 1902 upon the teleological possibilities within one rather specific but fertile metaphor. As long as Conrad can temper his analysis of the metaphysical emptiness at the heart of modern experience by developing characters capable of maturing insight, he avoids the depression that attaches to a character such as Willems, who is unable to navigate through the wilderness of the jungle or of his heart. In 1902, however, such tempering fails Conrad, and at that point, at least until he writes "The Secret Sharer" in 1908, he finally puts his metaphor of navigation to rest.

If only because it is the last of the tales in this early period of sea fiction, "The End of the Tether" becomes an especially crucial work in the whole of Conrad's writing career. It is evident from the emphasis that the narrator places upon Captain Whalley's past, a past in which he has been known as "Daredevil Harry Whalley, of the *Condor*, a famous clipper in her day" (p. 167), that the tale continues much of the metaphoric value in navigation that the earlier tales developed. In fact, when one recalls that this Whalley has been "the pioneer of new routes and new trades" and that he has "steered across the unsurveyed tracts of the South Seas, and [has] seen the sunrise on uncharted islands," one knows that he is even one of those very rare navigators in Conrad's fiction who have risen to the challenges of exploration and who thus, much like Captain Cook and Sir John Franklin, deserves the stature of representing the best in Western traditions of seamanship. That he enjoys such stature there should be little doubt, for as the narrator himself reminds us, "[Is] there not somewhere between Australia and China a Whalley Island and a Condor Reef?" (p. 168). Every detail about Whalley's professional past, even the other officers' awe before the rigorous routine that he follows each morning upon awakening, underscores the fact that this captain has gained the high esteem of his profession and is, therefore, the consummate navigator.

At the same time, nevertheless, while Whalley is a crack commander, and while he may thus seem to possess good reason to believe in the continued progress of his own career, the world in which Whalley has made his large reputation has changed dramatically with the opening of the Suez Canal in 1869 and especially with the introduction of steamers to the Far East. With those changes Whalley, who throughout his mature life has expected to go out decently in the end, suddenly discovers his life in sails as "an archaic curiosity of the Eastern waters, a screed traced in obsolete words" (p. 186). In fact, by the time he does join the world of steam by accepting the command of the *Sofala*, he has become even in the eyes of his friend Van Wyk "an amazing survival from the prehistoric times of the world" (p. 287). The point, of course, is not merely that Whalley has become old or superannuated, but that the whole scheme of values that has defined the old world of sailing no longer obtains, at least with its full force, in the world of steam. The Whalley who in the prime of his life was happy to hear of Elliott's promotion to master-attendant so that he — Whalley — can continue "to serve no one but his own auspicious fortune" (p. 196), is a captain who takes genuine delight in the wonderful possibilities both in his life of radical individualism and in his participation within a rich tradition that underlies and supports his association with several famous sailing ships. He is also the captain who in his retirement buys a barque, the *Fair Maid*, so that he can continue to nurture his dream of self-sufficiency and heroic grandeur. He has known, as few of his peers have, the craft of sailing in danger and uncertainty, at the whim of the wind and of fortune, and he has thrived upon the challenge. Now, however, with the increasing reliance upon steam in the Far East he suddenly finds himself, if not an outcast, at least a forgotten man with little to humor himself but his lingering indulgence of the *Fair Maid*.

That this shift from a world of sails to a world of steam is crucial to the story becomes apparent, early, when Whalley discovers that his daughter, Ivy (the name foreshadows the fact that she is about to choke her father), requires money because her husband has turned invalid. At that point the captain tries to turn his self-indulgence upon the *Fair Maid* into a profitable enterprise but learns that in the face of the more reliable steamer competition he can make little profit. The upshot of the dilemma is that when Ivy needs even more money for opening a boardinghouse, he finds that he has no alternative but to sell his treasured barque. The selling of the *Fair Maid*, however, is not the worst of the matter. Whalley, after thriving in an era when men and ships enlivened each other and when "individuals were of some account" (p. 193), now discovers that he must also join the company of men who "command" steamers. Such a shift is not easy, especially with the attitudes that Whalley has, understandably enough, allowed to crystallize. The narrator provides one particularly nice example of such crystallization:

> A laid-up steamer was a dead thing and no mistake; a sailing-ship somehow seems always ready to spring into life with the breath of the incorruptible heaven; but a steamer, thought Captain Whalley, with her fires out, without the warm whiffs from below meeting you in her decks, without the hiss of steam, the clangs of iron in her breast — lies there as cold and still and pulseless as a corpse. (P. 214)

It is true that Whalley regards the opportunity to serve on the *Sofala* as a godsend, particularly because he has already found the sale of the *Fair Maid* "involving [him in] a radically new view of existence" (p. 184) without honorable employment, but such regard must not result in the reader's ignoring the captain's deeper feelings when he joins the *Sofala*.

By joining the *Sofala* Whalley essentially experiences what Conrad himself endured as first mate aboard the *Vidar* from August to December 1887.[1] The monotonous course of the *Vidar* through the Malay Archipelago is Conrad's own introduction to steaming in the Far East, and it is probable that Whalley's attitudes toward his new experience of "steaming" are a reflection of Conrad's own disgust with his brief but demoralizing service upon a steamer. In fact, upon reading Conrad's letters or his nostalgic *The Mirror of the Sea*, which appears in serials during 1905-6, one can develop substantial evidence to demonstrate that Whalley's attitudes are rooted in Conrad's own disillusionment concerning the nature of "modern" sea experience. Throughout *The Mirror* especially, after noting how "the machinery, the steel, the fire, the steam have stepped in between the man and the sea" (*MS*, p. 72), Conrad repeatedly insists upon the fact that service upon a steamship is not an art. Here the passage from *The Mirror* that I quoted at greater length in chapter 5, and in which Conrad defines the nature of service upon a steamship, bears brief reconsidering: service upon steamers "is

less personal and a more exact calling; less arduous, but also less grati-
fying in the lack of close communion between the artist and the medium
of his art. It is, in short, less a matter of love'' (*MS*, p. 30). The contempt in the passage, of course, originates in the belief that service upon
a more ''manageable'' steamer is a diminishing of the art of navigation.
By now such contempt is hardly surprising, for throughout Conrad's
early sea fiction, but especially toward the end of the period (except
when Conrad is introducing the ambiguities of irony, as with Rout and
Falk), the genuine navigators tend to disdain service upon steamers.
Whalley, like the Marlow who is ambivalent about his shift from six
years of sailing in the Far East to steaming up the Congo River, is no
exception. In terms of the metaphor of navigation, he is by joining the
*Sofala* ''furling the sails'' of proud individualism and, consequently, is
gradually exposing himself to egregious self-contempt.

To be sure, even at age sixty-seven Whalley manages to keep the
*Sofala* on her regular course when her previous eleven captains had
failed. At the beginning of the story the narrator is distinctly appreciative of Whalley's achievement on his first steamer: ''She made her land-
falls to a degree of the bearing, and almost to a minute of her allowed
time. At any moment, as he sat on the bridge without looking up, or lay
sleepless in his bed, simply by reckoning the days and the hours he
could tell where he was — the precise spot of the beat'' (p. 166). Later
in the story the narrator also recounts how three years earlier Whalley,
in the presence of Van Wyk, made himself responsible for ''the regularity of the service'' (p. 285). Despite such appreciative overtones in the
narrator's appraisal of Whalley's *Sofala* stint, however, it is clear that
Whalley has compromised himself — if only in his imagination — by
accepting service upon a steamer.

The compromise is already apparent, as Lawrence Graver has pointed
out, in Whalley's deception of his old friend Elliott, first in relation to
Ivy's well-being, then in relation to his actual intentions concerning the
*Sofala* (Elliott does not realize that Whalley is desperate for a berth as
commander). Graver's comment is very illuminating: ''A character like
Whalley's cannot cease to be frank with impunity. . . . conceal-
ment . . . is weakness—it is deterioration.''[2] Then there is the compromise of the next morning when, after a night of reflection concerning Massy's attitudes, Whalley allows himself to enter into partner-
ship with such a marginal, almost crazed, owner whose additional status
as chief engineer (Massy is not another Rout) should itself be warning

enough. Part of this compromise is that the sober Whalley allows Massy to believe he has an alcohol problem, against which the scheming Massy has his lawyer draw up a clause in the contract. At the same time, because he is in the peak of health, and because he expects Providence to sustain him in his efforts to support Ivy, Whalley unwittingly compromises himself by ignoring the necessity on his own behalf of an illness clause as protection for the future. The result is that while Whalley need not fear litigation because of drinking, he makes himself vulnerable to, or dependent upon, Massy if he should become ill. Such vulnerability, of course, is a measure of the proud Whalley's deterioration, of his diminishing stature as a navigator who has become involved in a situation beyond his previous experience. Indeed, unlike Jukes's dependence upon MacWhirr or the young captain's upon Falk, neither of which prevent the two young men's growth and maturation, Whalley's dependence upon Massy (whose name signifies material) virtually guarantees the fact that he will be uprooted from a firm tradition of personal responsibility and glorious self-realization. It is when Whalley turns blind, and then becomes consciously disloyal to his craft because he cannot divulge his condition to Massy for fear of losing his investment in the *Sofala*, that he fully reveals the deterioration that now drains Conrad's metaphor of navigation of all its past force.

That it is Whalley's blindness that defines the extent of his deterioration becomes more apparent if one considers the essential structure of the story. The story begins with the *Sofala* approaching the bar leading into the river up to Batu Beru, the location of Van Wyk's plantation. It generally ends, the evening of the following day, with the *Sofala* disintegrating against the reefs that line the one-hundred-mile waterway toward Pangu Bay, a waterway that the narrator describes (as has already been noted) almost at the very middle of the tale. Such careful construction, and especially the firm concentration upon thirty-six hours of navigation (despite whatever necessary digressions the narrator must make), suggests that the narrator is pointing up the diminished stature of Whalley as the *Sofala* captain. For in these thirty-six hours the reader sees the blind Whalley nearly ground the *Sofala* in the mud when the Serang fails to line the steamer up with the opening through the bar near Batu Beru; and then he sees Whalley helpless, seized by "the horror of incertitude" (p. 328) when the *Sofala* ranges far off her course while steaming toward Pangu Bay. The Whalley who in this short time fails twice is obviously a seaman who has lost his confidence in his ability to navigate. One may initially wish to ascribe this loss to his waning eyesight, but one must also acknowledge the possible implication that it is Whalley's several compromises — and especially his uprooting from a long and precious sailing tradition — that have broken his health and confidence. In these terms, it is true, Whalley's blindness may even serve as a metaphor for Western man's spiritual decline. One passage, which appears when the captain tries himself to line the steamer up for passage through the bar near Batu Beru, is particularly revealing on this point: "Captain Whalley strode forward to the rail; but his eyes, instead of going straight to the point, with the assured keen glance of a sailor, wandered irresolutely in space, as though he, the discoverer of new routes, had lost his way upon this narrow sea" (p. 217). Here the decline in Whalley's stature, from a sailor and navigator of new and uncharted routes to an irresolute fraud in a world of diminished frontiers, probably defines not only his own deterioration but also the decline of modern man.

The sudden absence in "The End of the Tether" of positive value within the metaphor of navigation, in addition to signaling the end of Conrad's early period of sea fiction, probably suggests that the author had become dissatisfied with the teleological salvation he had provided characters such as the young Marlows — salvation dependent principally upon the achievement of the stature of navigator, whether upon the sea or in the wilderness of the Congo. In a letter to Ford Madox Ford, which dates on the basis of internal evidence to February or March 1902 (and thus before the composition of "Tether"), Conrad offers a penetrating insight into his then-present crisis in writing for *Blackwood's Magazine*: "I haven't a single notion in my head. The 'wonderfulness' you have suggested is nowhere for the moment. Blackness is the impression of life — past and future; and though it is no doubt true and correct one can hardly fabricate 'maga' stuff out of it. 'Tis too subtle. 'Taint raw enough."[3] Eventually, in order to gain relief from the problems that this crisis presented, Conrad turned to larger social themes in novels such as *Nostromo, The Secret Agent*, and *Under Western Eyes*. In 1902, however, he was still writing "Tether," a tale that continues to focus — like the other early sea tales — upon the potential in the individual for self-realization, but that—unlike the others—also reveals in its three principal characters a succumbing to the bleak vision of reality at the heart of Conrad's later social and political novels.

In a sense, the characterization of Whalley, Massy, and Sterne represents an ironic extension of the teleological significance inherent in the metaphor of navigation.[4] For just as the navigator, by virtue of his increased insight both into the demands of his profession and into the limitations of human experience, achieves a confidence in himself that largely guarantees the success of his future action, so each of these three characters displays a confidence of self that seems to entail something of heroic stature. Whalley, for instance, has determined that his life's significance centers upon providing for Ivy, and in his successive distresses he never wavers from delighting in his assured paternalism: "He considered he was reaping the true reward of his life by being thus able to produce on demand whatever was needed" (p. 175). Even Massy, despite his ambition "to do nothing, nothing whatever, and to have plenty of money to do it on" (p. 268), has determined that his life's significance centers upon winning the Manila lottery, which once before had changed at least the circumstances, if not the substance, of his life. Confidently, he awaits a new "triumph." Sterne, too, as he at one point informs Massy, focuses his interest in what is happening aboard the *Sofala* upon a strong desire: "I want to get on. I make no secret of it that I am one of the sort that means to get on" (p. 238). When he discovers Whalley's blindness, of course, his confidence immediately increases. With their sure sense of goals and objectives, all three of these characters seem to possess firm convictions concerning their genuine substance and self-worth. In the face of the stature of Conrad's previous heroes, however, such conviction and self-justification must strike the reader as terribly ironic.

The result of all this rather blatant inversion of the heroism inherent in Conrad's earlier use of navigational metaphor is that the narrator must devote a great deal of unrelieved attention to analyzing the three characters' increasing moral ambivalence as their visions of worth fail. The narrator of "Tether," unlike Conrad's previous narrators, is not providing a "solution" to the metaphysical problems raised in the novel. Instead of tempering Conrad's seemingly inescapable metaphysical darkness by focusing upon the achievement of a new, viable perspective, one that (as in so many of the previous tales) is actually contingent upon the characters' loss of self-worth, he concentrates upon the further incarceration of each of the major characters in a moral ambivalence that is actually an outgrowth of their foolish pursuits. Such concentration obviously reduces "Tether" to the status of being one of Conrad's darkest tales, but it also makes the tale the turning point between Conrad's heroic sea tales and his dark social and political fiction.

The narrator notes, for example, that the proud Whalley already suspects in himself a loss of "truth and dignity," or that he feels himself "corrupt to the marrow of his bones" (p. 214), immediately after concluding his haggling with Massy for service on the *Sofala*. Then he notes that Whalley, after having begun the charade that conceals his blindness, gradually becomes conscious of a self-disgust for having allowed himself "to tamper" (p. 300) both with his conscience and with his lifelong devotion to genuine seamanship. Finally, he points out how Whalley, under the increasing pressure of possible discovery, suddenly acknowledges that his love of providing for Ivy has led him into the sin of presumption against Providence; and thus how, with his "past of honour, of truth, of just pride" having faded into a "steadily darkening universe," Whalley is left only with the consciousness of "a sudden vertigo and an overwhelming terror" (p. 324). At that point the narrator's analysis of Whalley's increasing self-contempt has virtually reached its culmination. For now this once vigorous captain, despite realizing that he is helpless in a universe where prayers are no longer of any significance, displays a terrible ambivalence of moral spirit when he decides to continue his charade even until the very end. On the one hand, he has become conscious of himself as one who has "deceived the poorest sort of devil on earth" (p. 299), that is, Massy; and on the other, as one who must "cling to his deception with a fierce determination to carry it out to the end" (p. 324) in order to save Ivy's money. It is this ambivalence that shortly leads to the wreck of the *Sofala* and to Whalley's death by drowning, and that — at least within the context of Conrad's early sea fiction — also serves as the nadir of the heroic experience inherent in the navigation metaphor.

Whalley's self-contempt is unquestionably of a greater intensity than that of Massy and Sterne, and yet these two men of the sea are also vulnerable to serious doubt about themselves. Massy originally delights in owning the *Sofala* because as owner he, not the captain, becomes the ultimate superior on the ship. (Such status, it should be clear, completely inverts the traditions of seamanship.) At the same time, however, because he allows his slim profits to be eaten up by his lottery mania, and because he does not work hard at building up a successful trade for his steamer, he has gradually become conscious of his power as owner as virtually empty. Even then, nevertheless, despite his perplexing awareness of his own folly, and despite the fact that the *Sofala* has fallen into extreme disrepair and thus has become an albatross, he continues to fear "losing that position which [has] turned out not worth having" (p. 218). In fact, when Whalley informs him that he intends to leave his employ in six weeks, Massy becomes furious with worry about how he shall continue to keep the *Sofala* solvent and in repair. At that point his moral ambivalence toward his own status as owner quickly approaches its culmination as he begins to focus all his hate for his own impotence upon Whalley. On the one hand, he bitterly berates this captain who—like the power of ownership—has eluded his grasp; on the other, he desperately fears that this captain—and his money—will not remain in the *Sofala*'s service. The result of such ambivalence is that Massy cannot avoid, for days on end, the fact that he has become a "fool" for associating himself with an old run-down steamer. Such self-contempt, of course, ultimately leads to a bitterness of temperament that reduces his life to "a sort of inferno—a place where his lost soul has been given up to the torment of savage brooding" (p. 269). Even then, however, Massy's self-contempt reaches its final culmination only when he hangs his jacket with the soft iron near the binnacle and then prepares to squander his insurance money in the Manila lottery. By then, obviously, he represents the nadir of villainous experience in the early sea tales.

Sterne, too, with his strong desire for promotion, exposes himself to the possibility of self-contempt. Although one might initially expect (especially in the context of all the other young heroes in previous tales) this young mate to rise to the stature of captain-navigator in a moment of disaster or unexpected challenge, one must be careful to remember the narrator's warning that this mate's extreme desire for promotion makes him "instinctively disloyal" (p. 239) and thus unworthy material for a command. Furthermore, having noted that Sterne, much like Jim on the *Patna*, has not enjoyed a history of effective action, whether in the world of steam or in sails, one must from the beginning doubt whether this mate will ever succeed in turning his one supreme chance for a command into the desired end. Sterne is not of the mold of the young Marlows and the Jukes, and thus when he makes his discovery of Whalley's blindness but then—instead of acting in the best interests of the

*Sofala* — merely allows himself to consider at length the possibilities for his own promotion to command, one should not be surprised that his deliberations lead nowhere. Sterne may pride himself upon his "exceptional powers of observation" (p. 255), but, unlike a genuine navigator, he also trembles at the possibility that the disclosure of his staggering discovery on Massy's ship may become a torpedo: "It is the sort of weapon to make its possessor careworn and nervous. He had no mind to be blown up himself; and he could not get rid of the notion that the explosion was bound to damage him, too, in some way" (p. 252). The result of such trembling is that the self-interested Sterne delays and delays and ultimately never makes a substantial contribution to the navigation of the *Sofala* by exposing Whalley. Eventually, in fact, he becomes almost as morally ambivalent as Massy. As the narrator points out, the discovery of Whalley's blindness has served only to introduce Sterne to his own inferno of self-doubt: "No more idle, random thoughts; the discovery . . . [now] put them on the rack, till sometimes he wished to goodness he had been fool enough not to make it at all" (p. 247). Like Whalley and Massy, Sterne — despite his youth and apparent vigor — merely serves as another example of the moral ambivalence that is the antithesis of heroic navigation and that signals the end of Conrad's first great period of fiction.

If, then, Conrad was obsessed with "the blackness," as his February 1902 letter to Ford suggests, his portrayal of Whalley, Massy, and Sterne probably reflects his sudden but complete inability to develop an alternative to the moral reduction that had appeared throughout the period in the Beards and the Hermanns but that at this point completely dominated. Thereafter, instead of focusing upon the self-realization of the individual, Conrad would center his attention upon the insufficiency of the individual's perception or action within a larger social and mechanized landscape. Whether the man is Nostromo or Verloc or Razumov, Conrad's new "hero" would in no way enjoy the intensity of freedom and possibility that is, say, Marlow's when the captain leaves Jim in Patusan for the last time and again regains the sea: "I let my eyes roam through space, like a man released from bonds who stretches his cramped limbs, runs, leaps, responds to the inspiring elation of freedom. 'This is glorious!' I cried." Such feeling belongs only to the sea fiction before "The End of the Tether."

# 11

# Conclusion

Now that the discussion of the relationships between Conrad's attitudes concerning the traditions of the sea and his handling of the eight principal stories from his early sea fiction is complete, a new overview for the period is possible. If one recognizes how the past three chapters have tended to compare and contrast the late works in the period with the early, one may already have begun to grasp the fact that "Typhoon," "Falk: A Reminiscence," and "The End of the Tether" are essentially ironic reworkings, respectively, of *The Nigger of the "Narcissus,"* *Heart of Darkness,* and *Lord Jim.* The three earlier works, of course, contain their own ironies. After all, who can forget the dramatic irony in the *Narcissus's* crew's supposed rebirth when, toward the end of the voyage, they engage in bickering and fighting among themselves over whether Wait's death has exactly coincided with the shift in barometric pressure? Or who can disregard the skein of verbal and dramatic ironies that help define the extremity of Marlow's experience in the Congo, or the structural irony of the novel's final section in which a very shrewd and much matured Marlow plays down his own vision and suggests that it is Kurtz who has perceived the supreme vision? Or who can ignore, in *Lord Jim,* the structural irony in Marlow's portrayals of Stein and the French lieutenant—and even of Jim's Patusan conduct? And yet, in the face of the darker irony that permeates the three works toward the end of the period, the more "artistic" ironies in the earlier works enjoy less impact. There is a good reason for this.

From the very beginning of the period Conrad was especially bent upon establishing his new metaphor of navigation as his "solution" to the problems that man faces while inhabiting a world of moral darkness and aimlessness. In the character of Marlow especially, since Marlow from the time of his *Judea* days to the time of his Patusan visit ages about twenty years, Conrad provides a thorough and very serious portrayal of the successive maturations that man requires in order to "solve" the problems of inhabiting this modern world. At twenty Marlow absorbs the traditions of his craft and becomes patient and confident about the future; at thirty he absorbs the bewildering yet liberating fact of the illusory basis behind all moral experience; at forty he achieves a new understanding of the necessity, yet the inescapable limitation, of human relationships in a world where every man is finally responsible only for himself. In these terms, of course, Marlow virtually by himself establishes the seriousness of Conrad's quest in the earlier sea tales for an alternative to the paralysis of will that defines Almayer and Willems. With the ambiguous *Lord Jim,* the last of the Marlow tales, however, Conrad already begins to separate himself from the quest for a moral alternative. In that novel, particularly through the ironies that attach to Jim's supposed awakenings, he initiates a reconsideration and, perhaps, even an undercutting of the solution that to that point has been so painstakingly developed.

That *Lord Jim* is the turning point is probably most evident in the fact that Jim has allowed himself to drift from the world of sails, following his back injury due to a falling spar, to the easy world of the East and of the steamers that populate that world. Before Jim only the Marlow of the Congo has belonged to a steamer, and his is a special case because he accepts such an assignment only after six months' looking for respectable employment at sea—presumably in sails. After Jim, however, there appear Jukes and MacWhirr, then Falk, and finally Whalley as seamen associated with steam. This shift from sails to steam, from the world of traditions and craft to the world of machines and trust in the material, possesses vast significance, for in addition to revealing Conrad's increasing pessimism concerning the problems of inhabiting a modern world (and thus preparing for Conrad's imminent exploration of the dark world within his social and political fiction), it points up the principal irony that characterizes the latter half of the period: the fact that *navigation in steam* is nearly a contradiction in terms. To be sure, in these works one can locate a Rout and a Falk as exemplars of vision, but neither man, especially Rout, who is confined to his engine room, provides much sense of that genuine navigation that earlier in the period reflected Conrad's great tradition of seamanship. Falk may tow schooners and barques from their berths in the river to the outer reaches of the bay, but in no sense does he strike the reader as a grand navigator on the open sea in the tradition of Captain Cook. When he tows, he tows with a single-mindedness, with a gruffness that reveals not a devotion to the craft but a respect for the monopoly that he has built up over the years.

Beyond *Lord Jim*, from "Typhoon" to "Tether," then, Conrad does reconsider the solution that he worked out in the first half of the period. In "Typhoon," for example, instead of concentrating alone upon the possibilities for maturation in Jukes, Conrad reverses the nature of the relationship between Marlow and Jim and explores the irony in the imaginative Jukes's dependence upon the dull MacWhirr for his opportunity to grow. The result of such reversal is that Conrad suddenly creates a doubt about his previous paradigm of heroic maturation. Essentially, he is suggesting, in contrast to his portrayals of the Marlow whose successive maturations are largely self-contained, that Jukes cannot achieve confidence in his own seamanship without MacWhirr. Such a suggestion, given Conrad's persistent appreciation of his own growth at sea to the end of his life, is a radical idea, and it argues that Conrad had begun the process of reconsideration that finally doomed the fundamental paradigm of the period (except, perhaps, in "The Secret Sharer" and *The Shadow-Line*, both of which follow the moral and philosophical upheaval of Conrad evident in his fiction from *Nostromo* to *Under Western Eyes*). The Jukes who becomes conscious of "an access of confidence, a sensation that *came from outside* [from MacWhirr's presence] like a warm breath" (emphasis added), obviously does not enjoy the nearly unqualified, largely self-generated maturation of the young Marlows. Similarly, because the captain's growth of perspective in "Falk" is largely dependent upon that strange card game in which he recognizes how much he and Falk are alike, the reader must recognize that he, too, does not enjoy the wonderful privilege of, say, the Marlow who matures before he arrives at the Inner Station and there meets Kurtz. To be sure, this newly commissioned captain, by absorbing the fact of his similarity to Falk, and especially by absorbing the metaphysics that have necessitated Falk's unusual behavior, does enjoy a much more profound growth than does Jukes. He, nevertheless, unlike the

Marlow who is superior to Kurtz, is still dependent upon Falk for much of his illumination. By the time Whalley appears, of course, the doubts that are evident in Conrad's handling of Jukes and of the young captain achieve their fruition: Whalley, the representative of the old and grand tradition of seamanship, fails miserably before the economic and navigational pressures of modern, mechanized mercantile service. With Whalley the earlier doubts lie heavy, and ultimately Conrad sabotages the metaphor of self-realization at sea because the times no longer are propitious.

In addition to noting the tremendous, sometimes excruciating irony that characterizes Conrad's thematic reconsideration of his heroic paradigm from Jukes to Whalley, one must also recognize that "Typhoon," "Falk,"and "Tether" are reworkings of the plots in the earlier novels. The discussion in previous chapters has already pointed out how both "Typhoon," with its movement from verbal absurdity to the ravaging of the gale to the "mutinous" struggle of the coolies, and "Falk," with its captain essentially encountering a bewildering Congo experience, mirror, respectively, the essential plot progressions of *The Nigger of the "Narcissus"* and of *Heart of Darkness*. The relationship between "Tether" and *Lord Jim,* however, I have ignored. If Whalley is seen as an elder version of Marlow, nevertheless, the relationship becomes immediately clear. Both Whalley and Marlow are great navigators, men of exacting standards and of considerable professional success, and both become involved in relationships that threaten their status and even their self-conceptions. For just as Marlow becomes responsible for a deserter's fate and finds himself making excuses for that deserter until it becomes necessary to direct him on his own responsibility into Patusan, so Whalley becomes increasingly more responsible for his daughter after she has made a poor marriage. Whalley, however, never manages to terminate such an exhausting responsibility. His son-in-law's "punctuality in failure" and then the latter's turning invalid guarantees Whalley's continued support of the daughter—even after huge losses in stock devaluation ultimately force him to sell his beloved *Fair Maid*. The result is that he, unlike Marlow, remains confined within a paternalism that essentially nullifies the process of growth inherent in Conrad's earlier commitment to radical individualism. Whalley, like Marlow, confronts a choice—whether to support the *Fair Maid* and the ethic of self-responsibility or to support Ivy and the ethic of paternalism. Marlow finally would have chosen the *Fair Maid*. Whalley, however, chooses the other alternative: instead of acknowledging that his primary responsibility as a man lies in his own development of craft, he above all cherishes his ability to provide for his daughter. From the Marlow of *Lord Jim* to the Whalley of ''Tether,'' it is clear, Conrad travels a great distance. Because of the vitality inherent in the wonderful vision of self-responsibility that informs most of the period, most readers of Conrad may wish to side with Marlow as the superior of the two men, but here the very fact that Conrad travels in a direction even beyond Whalley, to the Verlocs and Razumovs, may indicate that Conrad himself is unsure which of the two men he prefers. The Marlow of *Lord Jim* is a marvelous seaman and a true friend, and yet he possesses a coldness of insight (witness all his shafts of irony while he listens to Jim's account of the *Patna* crisis) that sharply distinguishes his character from that of Whalley. Whalley probably enjoys fewer friends than does Marlow—after all, he does not have the advantage of such cleverness and wit—but he does possess a warmth that Conrad may now fully appreciate. If one recognizes anything at all here, then, one must consider the possibility that in the latter half of the period Conrad is tempering his vision of maturation into a life of self-responsibility. Perhaps with the three final tales he is recognizing that all men, especially in a new century, cannot be Marlows and that there is something wonderful, as well as tragic and ironic, in the fates of the MacWhirrs and Whalleys.

What happened to Conrad from 1897 to 1902 also bears brief consideration from an aesthetic perspective. Throughout the period Conrad continued and developed the Romantics' interest in exploring and dramatizing the thoughts and the feelings of man as he confronts those watersheds of experience which initiate in him change and self-realization. Perhaps this interest is most apparent in the dominant use of first-person narration during the period, especially the complicated use, again, of Marlow in the tales at the heart of the period. First-person narration obviously provides the Conrad who has been struggling to make concrete the psychological paralysis of Almayer or the bewildering passion of Willems with the means for much more adequately portraying the complex mixture of thought and emotion that defines a character's response to an immediate situation. With Marlow, for example, Conrad is able to develop a continuum of consciousness that chooses and arranges past events and circumstances and that, in doing so, creates a conception of those past events and circumstances with which he (or his image of himself) may be comfortable. It is true, of course, that if Marlow's is such a narrative situation, one can accuse him of merely "editing" or rationalizing his experience in order to fit whatever contours the present demands, but one can also regard him as one of the most important heroes of modern fiction in the sense that he may mature as a result of making his very subjective experiences of past thought and emotion the means to further self-knowledge beyond what he has already absorbed on the *Judea,* in the Congo, or in Patusan.

Such a phenomenological appraisal of the elder Marlow's verbal acts in the fiction at the heart of the period firmly establishes experience, whether physical or verbal or even preverbal, as the primary value of human existence in Conrad's fictional world, and thus while the reader may wish to argue—along with a host of critics—that self-knowledge is the determined goal of experience in Conrad's world, it may be more shrewd to argue that experience is sufficient in itself. With Conrad the moral question of self-knowledge is ultimately not a matter of developing consistent systems of ethics but of man's merely facing, because his perceptions are limited phenomenologically, the hazy dimensions of his experience as genuinely as he can. That is why the younger Marlow, in the Congo and traveling beyond the trammels of history and civilization, becomes such a great figure in the early Conrad: he sees as fully as he then can that the nameless, wordless, patternless wilderness enjoys no immediately apparent referent in the visualized, verbalized, categorized world of past social impressions. Such a perception, furthermore, by allowing him to consider the very rudiments of civilization, enables him to avoid the undistinguished, rote observance of social patterns by which so many of Conrad's other characters "imprison" themselves. Whether it is the younger or the older Marlow, both become the chief exhibits of the crucial importance in Conrad's early sea fiction of a commitment to genuine perception.

Because of this emphasis upon a narrator who has matured in the past and in the present by virtue of his commitment to as genuine a perception of his experience as he is capable of, Conrad finally makes the present verbal behavior of his speaker one of the primary keys to interpreting the fiction of this period. The fact that the reader cannot, in *Heart of Darkness,* ignore the narrating Marlow's tongue-in-cheek presentation of the spectacular quality within Kurtz's final perception argues that the reader's appraisal of this narrating Marlow is of nearly as much importance as his appraisal of the younger Marlow who penetrates into the heart of the Congo. Such preoccupation with the verbal act of the narrator should provide a clue to the essential ambiguity within all three of the Marlovian narrations. The Marlow of "Youth" may seem to cloud his narrative with nostalgia and rhapsodic reminiscing, or the Marlow of *Heart of Darkness* may avoid an explicit analysis of the superiority of his perceptions in the Congo to Kurtz's final insight, or the Marlow of *Lord Jim* may avoid explicit judgments of the French lieutenant and of Stein and even of Jim—but the reader can still, if he is attentive to Marlow's metaphors and ironies, determine what the captain's views and judgments are. In these terms, of course, Marlow's verbalizing, an act that illuminates at the same time that it obfuscates, becomes one of the most sophisticated and distinguished narratives in all modern fiction.

With the collapse in "Tether" of the navigational metaphor and thus of his intense appreciation of the individual's commitment to perception, Conrad suddenly found himself rather fully separated from that world in which the narrative act is at once a selective examination of the past but also a present assertion of the narrator's continued commitment to the genuineness of perception. In "Tether" and beyond, but with some qualification as in the narrative handling of *Under Western Eyes* and *The Shadow-Line,* Conrad returned to that third-person narration wherein the focus of the narrative is no longer rather equally divided between past event and present act but upon, say, the elaborate patterns of irony whereby the "meaning" of a novel such as *The Secret Agent* finally becomes evident. Instead of complicating the texture of his narrative by filtering all past events and circumstances through a present consciousness that is itself, no matter how slightly, tied to other events and circumstances, Conrad in later novels turned away from his earlier concentration upon the subjective character of all knowledge and increasingly turned to more objective and finally more conservative values in order to free himself of, and thus to give some moral focus to, the intellectual confusion that had thoroughly seized him by the time he tackled "Tether." "Tether" signals for Conrad the end of that introspective period in which he through Marlow and other first-person narrators sought to discover out of the past some meaningful values for the present. As long as Conrad limited himself in that period to an imaginative yet subjective rehearsal of the values (the crafts and the traditions of the sea) whereby he had himself, years ago, achieved a wonderfully meaningful existence, he managed to solve all the thematic and the narrative difficulties that the tales produced (with the possible exception of Falk's rehearsal of his cannibalism at the end of that story). Even with the consistent success of the period, however, and despite the marvelous success of ''Tether'' itself, Conrad with ''Tether'' exhausted his particularly fertile metaphor and his narrative framework. Thereafter, his fiction quickly took on altogether new thematic and narrative directions.

The fact that the Conrad between ''Tether'' and *Nostromo* experienced a huge shift in emphasis, loosely from a subjective vision to one that was more objective, parallels what many other writers in modern England have experienced. Joyce and Eliot, for example, with their constant evocation of classical and Christian humanism, sought to provide their contemporary life with an order or framework very different from that of the Romantics, whose interest was in dramatizing subjective thoughts and feelings. Even Yeats, who with his vision managed to create a perspective of somewhat exaggerated subjectivity, increasingly directed his late poetry into an exploration of that solar phase which he had associated with conservative, aristocratic values such as permanence and the appreciation of artifice. Lawrence, too, having written the psychoautobiographical *Sons and Lovers,* turned to an apocalyptic presentation of three generations in *The Rainbow* in order to contain that shift in modern sensibility toward undisciplined subjectivity which so much appalled him throughout his writing career. Finally, in fact, because such late writers as Forster and Woolf continued the reaction against exaggerated subjectivity that Conrad had begun in his fiction by 1902, one might properly regard—although I will not press the point —''The End of the Tether'' as something of a watershed in English Literature.

# Notes

**Chapter 1**      **Conrad's Essays: The Background behind His Early Sea Fiction**

1. Two books have recently appeared that at least begin to explore the possibilities of such an approach: C. F. Burgess's *The Fellowship of the Craft: Conrad on Ships and Seamen and the Sea* (Port Washington, N.Y.: Kennikat Press, 1976) and David Thorburn's *Conrad's Romanticism* (New Haven, Conn.: Yale University Press, 1974). Neither book, however, advances the larger critical relationships between Conrad's sea experience and his use of navigational metaphor that inform this study. Burgess merely sets forth the nature of Conrad's attitudes toward life at sea. Thorburn pursues more significant critical relationships, but his general thesis that Conrad's fiction is rooted in the tradition of adventure stories (and is thus romantic) prevents him from appreciating how influential the crisis between the world of sails and that of steam was for both Conrad the seaman and Conrad the novelist.

2. For parenthetical references within the text I have abbreviated these four volumes, respectively, to *MS, PR, NLL*, and *LE*. References to Conrad's writings throughout this book are to Dent's *Collected Edition of the Works of Joseph Conrad*, 21 vols. (London: J. W. Dent and Sons, 1946–55). Pagination is the same as in the Dent Uniform Edition (1923, 1926) and in the Doubleday, Page and Company Canterbury Edition (1924). For *Heart of Darkness*, however, I have used the Norton Critical Edition, edited by Robert Kimbrough (New York, 1971). For *Lord Jim*, again the Norton Critical Edition, edited by Thomas Moser (New York, 1968).

3. V. S. Naipaul, "Conrad's Darkness," *New York Review of Books*, 17 October 1974, p. 19.

4. For further facts concerning this period, see Jerry Allen, *The Sea Years of Joseph Conrad* (New York: Doubleday, 1965), app., "Conrad's Voyages," pp. 315–25.

5. There is some dispute whether this rescue occurred while Conrad was associated with the *Loch Etive*. See Allen, *Sea Years of Conrad*, pp. 117–20.

6. On this point, see Conrad, *A Personal Record,* p. 13, and Conrad, *Last Essays,* pp. 16 – 17. One might also recall in this connection the young Marlow's fascination with the blank spaces of the Congo — a fascination that has its basis in Conrad's own life.

7. This phrase is picked up, of course, from *Heart of Darkness:* the knights of the sea, Sir Francis Drake and Sir John Franklin among them, were "bearers of a spark from a sacred fire" (p. 4).

8. Again, for the facts on Conrad's berths in these steamers, see Allen, *Sea Years of Conrad,* app.

9. Finally, Conrad is even willing, as he points out in *The Mirror of the Sea,* to justify all sailing ships as ultimately redeemable: "For that the worst of [sailing] ships would repent if she were ever given time I make no doubt. I have known too many of them. No [sailing] ship is wholly bad; and now that their bodies that had braved so many tempests have been blown off the face of the sea by a puff of steam, . . . there can be no harm in affirming that in these vanished generations . . . there never has been one utterly unredeemable soul" (pp. 119–20). This quotation obviously defines the full extent of Conrad's exaggerated preference for sails.

10. Royal Roussel, *The Metaphysics of Darkness* (Baltimore, Md.: Johns Hopkins University Press, 1971), pp. 37–42.

### Chapter 2         *The Nigger of the "Narcissus"*: The New Metaphor

1. Conrad's essay "The Fine Art" is especially eloquent on this point. See Conrad, *The Mirror of the Sea,* pp. 23–35.

2. Conrad, *A Personal Record,* p. 117.

3. There are well over a dozen passages in which Donkin and his mates later assert their manhood. Donkin, for example, insists: "We are as good men as 'ee!" (p. 91); "They aint men 'ere. . . . I am a man. . . . I am a man. . . . Ain't we men?" (pp. 118–20); "Ye're no men!" (p. 136); "That's the man I am" (p. 153); "But I am a man" (p. 168). This insistence upon manhood, of course, intensifies the crew's pursuit of gentility.

4. Cf. Frederick R. Karl, *A Reader's Guide to Joseph Conrad* (New York: Noonday Press, 1960), p. 91.

5. Roussel, *Metaphysics of Darkness,* pp. 37–42.

6. James E. Miller, Jr., "*The Nigger of the 'Narcissus'*: A Re-examination," *PMLA* 66 (1951):913.

7. Norman Friedman, "Criticism and the Novel," *Antioch Review* 18 (1958): 368.

8. Cecil Scrimgeour, "Jimmy Wait and the Dance of Death: Conrad's *Nigger of the 'Narcissus,'*" *Critical Quarterly* 7 (1965):349.

### Chapter 3         Narrative Irony in "Karain: A Memory"

1. It is probably for this reason that Belfast reminds him at the end of the voyage, "You were his chum, too" (p. 171).

2. Almost all critics of *The Nigger of the "Narcissus"* have noted and even argued about the peculiar handling of narrative voice. Marvin Mudrick, in "The Artist's Conscience and *The Nigger of the 'Narcissus,'*" *Nineteenth-Century*

*Fiction* 11 (1957):295, disparages the handling of voice: "Conrad . . . is too taken with his metaphysics to go much beyond merely stating it, to aim at elaborating or examining character and incident beyond the static, repetitive point of illustration and symbol." Ian Watt, on the other hand, in "Conrad Criticism and *The Nigger of the 'Narcissus,'*" *Nineteenth-Century Fiction* 12 (1958):261, has justified such handling on the grounds that "the continual and immediate presence of an individualized narrator, sleeping in a certain bunk, of past and present circumstances, could not but deflect our attention from the book's real protagonist—the ship and its crew." Neither critic, however, fully explores the significance of the transition in narrative *voice*, both in person and in number. More recent critics, too, have avoided such an analysis.

3. See especially Bruce M. Johnson, "Conrad's 'Karain' and *Lord Jim,*" *Modern Language Quarterly* 24 (1963):13–20.

4. The phrase from *Heart of Darkness*, "a deaf and dumb universe," may be too strong for this discussion. Karain's moral categories are collapsing, but he is not entering Marlow's prehistoric wilderness where there exist no categories at all.

5. Albert J. Guerard, *Conrad the Novelist* (Cambridge, Mass.: Harvard University Press, 1958), p. 91.

6. Johnson, "Conrad's 'Karain,'" p. 20.

7. Ibid., p. 17.

8. Ibid., p. 20.

## Chapter 4    Conrad's "Youth": Problems of Interpretation

1. V. J. Emmett, Jr., "'Youth': Its Place in Conrad's *Oeuvre,*" *Connecticut Review* 4, no. 1 (1970):55.

2. Another example of a critic who has probably yielded to the same temptation is Leo Gurko, who in *Joseph Conrad: Giant in Exile* (New York: Macmillan Co., 1962), p. 79, has argued that the young Marlow enjoys a "psychic" journey "from *youth* to *middle age*" (emphasis added).

3. Walter F. Wright, *Romance and Tragedy in Joseph Conrad* (Lincoln: University of Nebraska Press, 1949), p. 11. Albert Guerard, too, in *Conrad the Novelist,* p. 17, has concluded that "Youth" is "only [a] personal story in which the would-be initiate learns nothing, being still too young to learn."

4. Murray Krieger, "Conrad's 'Youth': A Naive Opening to Art and Life," *College English* 20 (1959):279. For other discussions of the elder Marlow's skepticism, see John H. Wills, "A Neglected Masterpiece: Conrad's Youth,'" *Texas Studies in Literature and Language* 4 (1963):591–601, and especially Stanton de Voren Hoffman, *Comedy and Form in the Fiction of Joseph Conrad* (The Hague: Mouton, 1969), pp. 99–107.

5. In a modest revision of his article, in *The Play and Place of Criticism* (Baltimore, Md.: Johns Hopkins Press, 1967), p. 96, Krieger makes his view very definite: "In *Youth* there is resistance to choice between the romantic striving [of the young Marlow] that may from a more sober view seem essentially aimless and the sensible compromise with reality [of the elder Marlow] that speaks of an inglorious weariness even as it boasts of wisdom."

6. There are roughly six episodes: the gale near Yarmouth Roads, the collision in the Tyne, the storm off the Lizards, the six-month delay in Falmouth, the explosion in the Indian Ocean, and the arrival in the East.

7. What happens to Abraham the steward and to Beard the captain during the course of the *Judea's* voyage is very illuminating on the point of madness.

8. Such a discovery is also the basis for the elder Marlow's later appreciation of the *Judea* sailors' "right stuff." With the passing of time, Marlow sympathizes with the hard cases who have joined the *Judea* and who have in them that "something solid like a principle" (p. 28) that enables them to meet the various challenges of the explosion in the Indian Ocean.

9. Significantly, this ripening is actually framed by the young Marlow's other maturations off the Lizards and in the Indian Ocean.

### Chapter 5        Navigation in *Heart of Darkness*

1. Kenneth Bruffee, "The Lesser Nightmare: Marlow's Lie in *Heart of Darkness*," *Modern Language Quarterly* 25 (1964):322–23.

2. James Guetti, *The Limits of Metaphor: A Study of Melville, Conrad, and Faulkner* (Ithaca, N.Y.: Cornell University Press, 1967), pp. 46–68. For another, more recent discussion of language in this novel, see Jerry Wasserman, "Narrative Presence: The Illusion of Language in *Heart of Darkness*," *Studies in the Novel* 6 (1974):327–38.

3. Bruce M. Johnson, *Conrad's Models of Mind* (Minneapolis: University of Minnesota Press, 1971), p. 88.

4. See especially Conrad's late essay, "Geography and Some Explorers," in *Last Essays*, pp. 1–21.

5. This passage has a strong parallel in Conrad's own life. See Conrad, "Geography and Some Explorers," pp. 16–17; see also Conrad, *A Personal Record*, p. 13.

6. It is probably true, however, that Marlow never entered the Congo with the idea of advancing that particular state of human knowledge.

7. Wylie Sypher, *Loss of the Self in Modern Literature and Art* (New York: Random House, 1962), pp. 58–59.

8. Earlier, on his passage to the Congo, Marlow already responded with delight to two "natural" rhythms: that of the surf and that of the natives who row out to the steamer. Such responses foreshadow his later respect for the cannibals.

9. The image of bloody shoes also has significance beyond indicating Marlow's "death." It points to the fact that Marlow will throw off Fresleven's shoes (the shoes of the previous captain) and thus will put on his own as a mature and responsible captain-helmsman. Later, when Marlow gives the harlequin a pair of shoes, the image reaches its ultimate significance: when the harlequin leaves with Marlow's pair of shoes, one must anticipate — if one can rely upon a consistency of metaphor — that this harlequin still has much to learn about the wilderness and about himself. In fact, as long as he wears Marlow's shoes, he shall not enjoy full maturity of insight.

10. In this connection, too, one might recall Fresleven: Fresleven dies because he "probably felt the need at last of asserting his self-respect in some way" (p. 9) during a dispute with some natives over two black hens.

### Chapter 6　　Lord Jim (I): Marlow's Interviews with Jim and with Jewel

1. See, for example, John Palmer, *Joseph Conrad's Fiction* (Ithaca, N.Y.: Cornell University Press, 1968), pp. 34–35. Guerard, too, in *Conrad the Novelist*, p. 126 ff., discusses at length Conrad's use of impressionism.

2. Captain Brierly, of course, first proposes this possible course of action to Marlow.

3. Guerard, *Conrad the Novelist*, p. 152, suggests that Marlow's essential task is "to achieve a right human relationship with [Jim]. . . . Marlow must resist an excessive identification; . . . he must maintain a satisfactory balance of sympathy and judgment." At first one may wish to agree with Professor Guerard, but given the fact that Marlow does identify himself with Jim, Marlow's actual task in the novel is to discover the possibilities and the limitations of human relationships.

4. Mircea Eliade, *Myth and Reality* (New York: Harper Torchbooks, 1968), p. 131.

5. Elliott B. Gose, Jr., "Pure Exercise of Imagination: Archetypal Symbolism in *Lord Jim*," *PMLA* 79 (1964):137–47.

6. Leo Gurko, *Joseph Conrad*, p. 108, among others, has argued that in Patusan Jim eventually "has friends, enemies, responsibilities, a woman who loves him, and whom he loves, a fixed place in the world, and the sense of achievement that comes when the gap between the real self and the ideal disappears." The fact, however, that Jim here remains prey to the unpredictability of impulse must cloud with suspicion all his later achievements in Patusan.

7. A host of critics have argued the significance of Jim's final act. The vast majority avoid the view that the act is tantamount to suicide. Walter Wright, *Romance and Tragedy in Conrad*, p. 121, for example, suggests that Jim "cannot, till the end, immerse; and, when he does, he has learned to do so independently, not with the help of Stein." At least Gurko, *Joseph Conrad*, p. 111, has recognized the irony in the act: "Jim's capacity to sacrifice the concrete for the abstract, the real for the ideal, the living tissue of emotion for the veiled and inscrutable dream, removes him from the dimension of love and identification altogether and thrusts him, instead, into the harsh, bracing light of ironic definition." The full nature of that irony should now be very apparent.

8. The irony in this passage is that Marlow has frequently dealt in such shafts while listening to Jim's account of the *Patna* crisis. Now, however, having recognized the problems of such dealing, he avoids a tone of self-indulgence and quickly tries to face up to Jewel's need.

9. Critics of *Lord Jim* have singularly avoided arguing a maturation in Marlow himself. Only Daniel Schwarz, "The Journey to Patusan: The Education of Jim and Marlow in Conrad's *Lord Jim*," *Studies in the Novel* 4 (1972):442–58, has persuasively begun to present such a case.

10. That this is the point of suicide needs stressing. One of the important thematic unities in the last half of the novel is Conrad's ironic handling of suicide. On the one hand, Jim *seems* to trot off to a heroic death but virtually commits suicide; on the other, a despairing Marlow flirts with suicide yet finally recovers the vitality of his life at sea.

11. Perhaps because they have not perceived a maturation in Marlow, critics of *Lord Jim* have generally ignored the implications in the fact that Marlow ends his narrative before the conclusion of the novel. Like many of them, John Palmer, *Joseph Conrad's Fiction,* p. 39, merely concludes that "much of the material in the second half of the book does seem defiantly, sometimes almost comically, to resist integration into its central idea." Such a suggestion, of course, must be resisted.

### Chapter 7        *Lord Jim* (II): Marlow's Interviews with the Lieutenant and with the Philosopher

1. Concerning the lieutenant, Dorothy Van Ghent, *The English Novel: Form and Function* (New York: Harper Torchbooks, 1961), p. 231, has argued that he is "the only character in the book in whom we can read the stamp of the author's own practical 'approval.' " Guerard, *Conrad the Novelist,* p. 157, regards him as "a moving figure of professional competence and integrity, and a man certainly capable of sympathy." Gurko, *Joseph Conrad*, p. 107, makes the lieutenant's commentary on fear the virtual key to interpreting the whole novel. Only Paul Kirschner, *Conrad: The Psychologist as Artist* (Edinburgh: Oliver & Boyd, 1968), p. 53, who regards the officer as a "rank-and-file dogmatist," and W. F. Bolton, "The Role of Language in *Lord Jim,*" *Conradiana* 1, no. 3 (1969):56, argue the alternative case. Bolton's view is fairly close to my own: "So far from being a man of discrimination, the French officer, the automaton of *la gloire*, is wholly unable to discern anything of [Jim's] case: for him 'the honour' alone is real." Bolton, however, does not expose the full texture of subtlety within Marlow's handling of the interview with the lieutenant.

Concerning Stein, Dorothy Van Ghent again, *The English Novel*, p. 242, has argued that Stein is a "hero of the intellect, and, in his way, a psychologist, a philosopher, and an artist." Guerard, *Conrad the Novelist,* p. 145, calls him a "meditative idealist who is also capable of action." John Palmer, *Joseph Conrad's Fiction*, p. 30, regards him as "a Renaissance man, a godlike figure created nowhere else in Conrad's fiction." Only Marian Brady, "The Collector-Motif in *Lord Jim,*" *Bucknell Review* 16 (1968):71, has shown any real sign of dissatisfaction with such a view of Stein: "Stein's inadequacy as a physician for Jim, and as a commentator on life and truth, is emphasized by the environment in which he lives. His entire collection is a celebration of immobility and death, his house a huge catacomb. . . . Shut up in the solitude of his house, Stein has dropped out of the comprehensive unity of mankind." In my examination of Marlow's interview with Stein I shall build upon Brady's insight.

2. The importance of such physical stolidity becomes even more obvious if one recalls Marlow's parallel, but blatant and rather grotesque, description of

the German captain's flight from further inquiry into the *Patna* affair.

3. This is the comment that Gurko, *Joseph Conrad*, p. 107, regards as the center of the novel. As he says, it provides "a thread that leads us through the mazes of the labyrinth to an ultimate clarity." Conrad himself, however, is probably investing the passage with terrible irony.

4. Such a gathering against the lieutenant makes the consensus of critical appreciation for this officer even more curious.

5. For further examination of Marlow's initial qualifications of Stein's Stature and commentary, see my discussion of the "frame" for the interview in "Marlow's Interview with Stein: The Implications of the Metaphor," *Studies in the Novel* 5 (1973):491 – 503.

6. For further discussion of the thematic overtones in the butterfly image, see Tony Tanner, "Butterflies and Beetles — Conrad's Two Truths," *Chicago Review* 16 (1963):123 – 40.

7. See Guerard, *Conrad the Novelist*, pp. 164 – 66; Robert Penn Warren, Introduction to *Nostromo*, by Joseph Conrad (New York: Modern Library, 1951), pp. xxi – xxiii.

8. It is interesting to note that Marlow conceives of Stein as hovering in the air, not swimming at the surface. The distinction might suggest that Stein can never again, himself, be immersed in the turbulence of the sea, although it is also true that hovering has connotations of staying close to the surface. Here the implications of the metaphor are very subtle, and yet Marlow's "intention" is probably apparent: he expects the reader to see Stein as a character with a fundamental weakness that mirrors Lord Jim's. Just as Jim confines himself to the airy dreams of heroism, so Stein tends to confine himself to spectacular dreams of beauty and harmony. The similarity becomes more apparent when the reader juxtaposes their retreats into passivity following the intrusion of a desperate Gentleman Brown and then of a grieving Jewel into their respective dreams. Like the fleeing Jim, Stein is never able, once he has fled Celebes and especially following his interview with Jewel, to return fully to the dramatic turmoils of surface swimming. In this scene, nevertheless, he is at least hovering.

### Chapter 8        "Typhoon": Ironic Diminishing of the Pattern

1. All the relationships in previous tales, such as between Lingard and Almayer (or Willems), or between the crew of the *Narcissus* and Wait (or Donkin), or between Karain and the white sailors, are merely pale shadows of the full-fledged relationship between Marlow and Jim.

2. Guerard, *Conrad the Novelist*, p. 294.

3. Jocelyn Baines, *Joseph Conrad: A Critical Biography* (London: Weidenfeld & Nicolson, 1960), p. 257.

4. Many critics in the past have argued that MacWhirr is one of Conrad's early heroes. Gurko, *Joseph Conrad*, p. 90, for example, has suggested that "MacWhirr is right on every count, and 'Typhoon' turns out to be a paean in his honor. The man without brains emerges, unexpectedly, as the voice of reason." Such a view, however, as shall be seen, is very wide of the mark.

5. Because Jukes' maturation in "Typhoon" is not as extreme as, say, Marlow's in the Congo, this emphasis upon imagery of hell or of the inferno seems a bit unwarranted. Finally, one of the crucial critical questions that must be addressed concerning this short novel is this: if Jukes's maturation is qualified, if it is slight compared to Marlow's, why does the narrator (Conrad) invest so much energy in presenting a whole series of terrifying moments for the young mate? Jukes in his own way seems to endure nearly as much harrowing experience as do a number of Conrad's other early heroes, and yet he does not mature as much. A good response to the question may simply be that Jukes's distress occurs during a period of less than a day while Marlow's, at least in the Congo, stretches over a period of several months. While Jukes is hardly given a chance to assimilate his experience, Marlow enjoys a much longer period in which to absorb the implications of his perceptions, and thus it is hardly surprising that his — Marlow's — maturation is so tremendous. From this perspective, of course, Jukes becomes a victim of narrative manipulations.

6. The narrator between the last two chapters of the novel entirely glosses over the second half of the typhoon. In the last chapter he simply recounts, much like the narrator of *The Nigger of the "Narcissus,"* the *Nan-Shan*'s arrival in Fu-chau.

7. Ted E. Boyle, *Symbol and Meaning in the Fiction of Joseph Conrad* (The Hague: Mouton, 1965), pp. 124–25, has even argued that upon the subsiding of the typhoon, Jukes loses the perception he has recently gained and thus has not changed.

8. Curiously (and I cite the comment only because it is indicative of the critical confusion concerning "Typhoon"), Walter Wright, *Romance and Tragedy in Conrad*, p. 13, has suggested that "of the three main characters — MacWhirr, the middle-aged Rout, and Jukes — Jukes is the only one not much changed at the end." Such a comment requires drastic revision in view of the new themes and ironies that have been established for the tale in the present discussion.

### Chapter 9  "Falk": The Last Maturation

1. For further information on this period in Conrad's life, see Baines, *Joseph Conrad*, pp. 87–92.

2. Conrad's earlier critics were largely critical of the tale. Baines points out that Conrad himself thought highly of the story, and he thus suggests that "it is certainly one of his best short stories" (ibid., p. 265). Guerard, *Conrad the Novelist*, p. 20, however, finds the story "diffuse" and "uninteresting." Moser, *Joseph Conrad*, p. 100, is even more critical: "Uncertainty of tone, particularly in Conrad's attempts to combine comic and serious elements, . . . makes the story unconvincing as art. Throughout, the narrator can only assert his feelings and ideas rather than dramatize them."

More recently, Bruce Johnson, "Conrad's 'Falk': Manuscript and Meaning," *Modern Language Quarterly* 26 (1965):276, has argued that the story "is ill-suited for the intellectual and emotional burden it simultaneously carries and avoids." John Palmer, *Joseph Conrad's Fiction*, p. 86, on the other hand, has called the tale "a minor-key masterpiece." It is with the discussions of Daniel Schwarz, "The Significance of the Narrator in Conrad's 'Falk: A Reminiscence,' " *Tennessee Studies in Literature* 16, (1971):103 – 10, and Joel Kehler, "The Centrality of the Narrator in Conrad's 'Falk,' " *Conradiana* 6 (1974):19 – 30, however, that the tale has begun to gain its proper focus — as another tale of significant maturation. By relating the tale to the larger context of Conrad's early sea fiction, and especially by concentrating upon the precise nature of the young captain's maturation, it is possible to reach an even fuller appreciation of the tale's subtle focus than that provided by these two critics.

3. Too often, having recognized the similarity in narrative situations between "Falk" and the Marlow tales, Conrad's readers have expected the narrator of "Falk" to recover Marlow's spirit and manner. Such an expectation, however, can only demean this narrator's stature. It is necessary to give him his own due, that is, to recognize his own style, and to do so one must at least accept the fact that in the three tales following *Lord Jim* Conrad's interest is not so much in the intriguing possibilities of Marlovian narrative as in the challenging juxtaposition of self-realization with the world of steam. The narrator of "Falk" is subtle, perhaps not as subtle as Marlow, but still very shrewd in his recognition of the vast change in himself that occurs as a result of his relationship with Falk.

4. A good deal of the critical confusion concerning "Falk" has resulted from the failure of critics to recognize the precise nature and purpose of this narrative complication. Some critics have argued that the story is about the captain's relationship to Falk; others, that it is about the captain's rise to new stature. Only Schwarz and Kehler have glimpsed the real narrative situation.

5. Schwarz, "Significance of the Narrator in 'Falk,' " p. 104.

6. Ibid.

7. In an era of various game theories, particularly of transactional analysis, the use of *game* as a critical metaphor may be misleading. Suffice it to say that Conrad himself uses the term, both in relation to the interview between the narrator-captain and Falk (p. 199) and in relation to the struggle between the carpenter and Falk on the *Borgmester Dahl* (p. 233). It seems, therefore, beyond question both that Conrad is using the metaphor to suggest a relationship between the captain-narrator and Falk and that this relationship consists in the similarity of the two men's perception of the game's significance.

**Chapter 10**     **"The End of the Tether": Teleological Diminishing in Conrad's Early Metaphor of Navigation**

1. For further information on this point, see Baines, *Joseph Conrad*, pp. 87 – 92.

2. Lawrence Graver, "Critical Confusion and Conrad's 'The End of the Tether,' " *Modern Fiction Studies* 9 (1964):391.

3. The letter is quoted by Douglas Goldring, *The Last Pre-Raphaelite* (London: MacDonald, 1948), p. 82.

4. For this very reason one must resist the curious critical tendency, somewhat prompted by Conrad himself when he includes the story in a volume with

"Youth" and *Heart of Darkness*, to concentrate upon the "unities" within the three stories. Critics may find some unities such as the progression from youth to old age, but the essential fact of the volume is that there is a tremendous difference in authorial attitude from the first story to the last. The Marlow of the first two stories is, therefore, better compared and contrasted to the Marlow of *Lord Jim* than to this Whalley, who becomes the victim of fundamental changes in navigation and especially of his own folly.

# Selected Bibliography

Allen, Jerry. *The Sea Years of Joseph Conrad*. Garden City, N.Y.: Doubleday and Company, 1965.

————. *The Thunder and the Sunshine*: *A Biography of Joseph Conrad*. New York: G. P. Putnam's Sons, 1958.

Aubrey, Georges Jean. *Joseph Conrad: Life and Letters*. 2 vols. Garden City, N.Y.: Doubleday, Page and Company, 1927.

————. *The Sea Dreamer: A Definitive Biography of Joseph Conrad*. Translated by Helen Sebba. Garden City, N.Y.: Doubleday, 1957.

Baines, Jocelyn. *Joseph Conrad*: *A Critical Biography*. London: Weidenfeld & Nicolson, 1960.

Biles, Jack I. "'Its Proper Title': Some Observations on *The Nigger of the 'Narcissus.'*" *Polish Review* 20, nos. 2-3 (1975):181–88.

Bolton, W.F. "The Role of Language in *Lord Jim.*" *Conradiana* 1, no. 3 (1969):51–59.

Boyle, Ted. E. *Symbol and Meaning in the Fiction of Joseph Conrad*. The Hague: Mouton, 1965.

Brady, Marian. "The Collector-Motif in *Lord Jim.*" *Bucknell Review* 16 (1968):66–85.

Bruffee, Kenneth. "The Lesser Nightmare: Marlow's Lie in *Heart of Darkness.*" *Modern Language Quarterly* 25 (1964):322–29.

Bruss, Paul S. "'Marlow's Interview with Stein: The Implications of the Metaphor.'" *Studies in the Novel* 5 (1973):491–503.

Burgess, C. F. *The Fellowship of the Craft: Conrad on Ships and Seamen and the Sea*. Port Washington, N.Y.: Kennikat Press, 1976.

Conrad, Jessie. *Joseph Conrad and His Circle*. London: Jarrolds Publishers, 1935.

———. *Joseph Conrad as I Knew Him*. Garden City, N.Y.: Doubleday, Page and Company, 1927.

Conrad, Joseph. *Collected Edition of the Works of Joseph Conrad*. 21 vols. London: J.W. Dent and Sons, 1946–55.

———. *Heart of Darkness*. Edited by Robert Kimbrough. New York: Norton, 1971.

———. *Lord Jim*. Edited by Thomas Moser. New York: Norton, 1968.

Eliade, Mircea. *Myth and Reality*. New York: Harper Torchbooks, 1968.

Emmett, V.J., Jr. " 'Youth': Its Place in Conrad's *Oeuvre*." *Connecticut Review* 4 no. 1 (1970):49–58.

Fleishman, Avrom. *Conrad's Politics: Community and Anarchy in the Fiction of Joseph Conrad*. Baltimore, Md.: Johns Hopkins Press, 1967.

Friedman, Norman. "Criticism and the Novel." *Antioch Review* 18 (1958):366–70.

Goldring, Douglas. *The Last Pre-Raphaelite*. London: MacDonald, 1948.

Gordon, John Dozier. *Joseph Conrad: The Making of a Novelist*. Cambridge, Mass.: Harvard University Press, 1940.

Gose, Elliott B., Jr. "Pure Exercise of Imagination: Archetypal Symbolism in *Lord Jim*." *PMLA* 79 (1964):137–47.

Graver, Lawrence. *Conrad's Short Fiction*. Berkeley: University of California Press, 1969.

———. "Critical Confusion and Conrad's 'The End of the Tether.' " *Modern Fiction Studies* 9 (1964):390–93.

Guerard, Albert J. *Conrad the Novelist*. Cambridge, Mass.: Harvard University Press, 1958.

Guetti, James. *The Limits of Metaphor: A Study of Melville, Conrad, and Faulkner*. Ithaca, N.Y.: Cornell University Press, 1967.

Gurko, Leo. *Joseph Conrad: Giant in Exile*. New York: Macmillan Co., 1962.

Harkness, Bruce, ed. *Conrad's "Heart of Darkness" and the Critics*. San Francisco: Wadsworth, 1960.

Haugh, Robert F. *Joseph Conrad: Discovery in Design*. Norman: University of Oklahoma Press, 1957.

Hay, Eloise Knapp. *The Political Novels of Joseph Conrad*. Chicago: University of Chicago Press, 1963.

Hewitt, Douglas. *Conrad: A Reassessment*. Cambridge: Bowes and Bowes, 1952.

Hoffman, Stanton de Voren. *Comedy and Form in the Fiction of Joseph Conrad*. The Hague: Mouton, 1969.

Hueffer, Ford Madox. *Joseph Conrad: A Personal Remembrance*. Boston: Little, Brown, 1924.

Johnson, Bruce M. "Conrad's 'Falk': Manuscript and Meaning." *Modern Language Quarterly* 26 (1965):267–84.

———. "Conrad's 'Karain' and *Lord Jim*." *Modern Language Quarterly* 24 (1963):13–20.

———. *Conrad's Models of Mind*. Minneapolis: University of Minnesota Press, 1971.

Karl, Frederick R. *A Reader's Guide to Joseph Conrad*. New York: Noonday Press, 1960.

Kehler, Joel. "The Centrality of the Narrator in Conrad's 'Falk.'" *Conradiana* 6 (1974):19–30.

Kirschner, Paul. *Conrad: The Psychologist as Artist*. Edinburgh: Oliver & Boyd, 1968.

Kramer, Dale. "Marlow, Myth, and Structure in *Lord Jim*." *Criticism* 8 (1966):263–79.

Krieger, Murray. "Conrad's 'Youth': A Naive Opening to Art and Life." *College English* 20 (1959):275–80.

———. *The Play and Place of Criticism*. Baltimore, Md.: Johns Hopkins Press, 1967.

Leavis, F.R. *The Great Tradition: George Eliot, Henry James, Joseph Conrad*. London: Chatto and Windus, 1948.

Malbone, Raymond Gates. " 'How to Be': Marlow's Quest in *Lord Jim*." *Twentieth Century Literature* 10 (1965):172–80.

Meyer, Bernard C., M.D. *Joseph Conrad: A Psychoanalytic Biography*. Princeton, N.J.: Princeton University Press, 1967.

Miller, J. Hillis. *Poets of Reality: Six Twentieth-Century Writers*. Cambridge, Mass.: Belknap Press, 1965.

Miller, James E., Jr. "*The Nigger of the 'Narcissus'*: A Reexamination." *PMLA* 66 (1951):911–18.

Morf, Gustav. *The Polish Heritage of Joseph Conrad*. London: Sampson, Low, Marston & Co., 1930.

Moser, Thomas. *Joseph Conrad: Achievement and Decline*. Cambridge, Mass.: Harvard University Press, 1957.

Mudrick, Marvin. "The Artist's Conscience and *The Nigger of the 'Narcissus*.'" *Nineteenth-Century Fiction* 11 (1957):288–97.

Naipaul, V.S. "Conrad's Darkness." *New York Review of Books*, 17 October 1974, pp. 16–21.

Palmer, John. *Joseph Conrad's Fiction*. Ithaca, N.Y.: Cornell University Press, 1968.

Rosenfield, Claire. *Paradise of Snakes: An Archetypal Analysis of Conrad's Political Novels*. Chicago: University of Chicago Press, 1967.

Roussel, Royal. *The Metaphysics of Darkness*. Baltimore, Md.: Johns Hopkins University Press, 1971.

Said, Edward W. *Joseph Conrad and the Fiction of Autobiography*. Cambridge, Mass.: Harvard University Press, 1966.

Schwarz, Daniel. "The Journey to Patusan: The Education of Jim and Marlow in Conrad's *Lord Jim*." *Studies in the Novel* 4 (1972):442–58.

————. " 'A Lonely Figure Walking Purposefully': The Significance of Captain Whalley in Conrad's 'The End of the Tether.' " *Conradiana* 7 (1975):165–73.

————. "The Significance of the Narrator in Conrad's 'Falk: A Reminiscence.' " *Tennessee Studies in Literature* 16 (1971):103–10.

Scrimgeour, Cecil. "Jimmy Wait and the Dance of Death: Conrad's *Nigger of the 'Narcissus.'* " *Critical Quarterly* 7 (1965):339–52.

Sherry, Norman. *Conrad and His World*. London: Thames and Hudson, 1973.

————. *Conrad's Eastern World*. Cambridge: At the University Press, 1966.

Stallman, Robert W., ed. *The Art of Joseph Conrad: A Critical Symposium*. East Lansing: Michigan State University Press, 1960.

Stevenson, Richard C. "Stein's Prescription of 'How to Be' and the Problem of Assessing Lord Jim's Career." *Conradiana* 7 (1976):233–43.

Sypher, Wylie. *Loss of the Self in Modern Literature and Art*. New York: Random House, 1962.

Tanner, Tony. "Butterflies and Beetles—Conrad's Two Truths." *Chicago Review* 16 (1963):123–40.

Thorburn, David. *Conrad's Romanticism*. New Haven, Conn.: Yale University Press, 1974.

Van Ghent, Dorothy. *The English Novel : Form and Function*. New York: Harper Torchbooks, 1961.

Warren, Robert Penn. Introduction to *Nostromo*, by Joseph Conrad. New York: Modern Library, 1951, pp. vii–xxxix.

Wasserman, Jerry. "Narrative Presence: The Illusion of Language in *Heart of Darkness*." *Studies in the Novel* 6 (1974):327–38.

Watt, Ian. "Conrad Criticism and *The Nigger of the 'Narcissus.' "* *Nineteenth-Century Fiction* 12 (1958):257–83.

Wegelin, Christof. "MacWhirr and the Testimony of the Human Voice." *Conradiana* 7 (1975):45–50.

Wiley, Paul L. *Conrad's Measure of Man.* Madison: University of Wisconsin Press, 1954.

Wills, John H. "A Neglected Masterpiece: Conrad's 'Youth.' " *Texas Studies in Literature and Language* 4 (1963):591–601.

Wright, Walter F. *Romance and Tragedy in Joseph Conrad.* Lincoln: University of Nebraska Press, 1949.

# Index

183